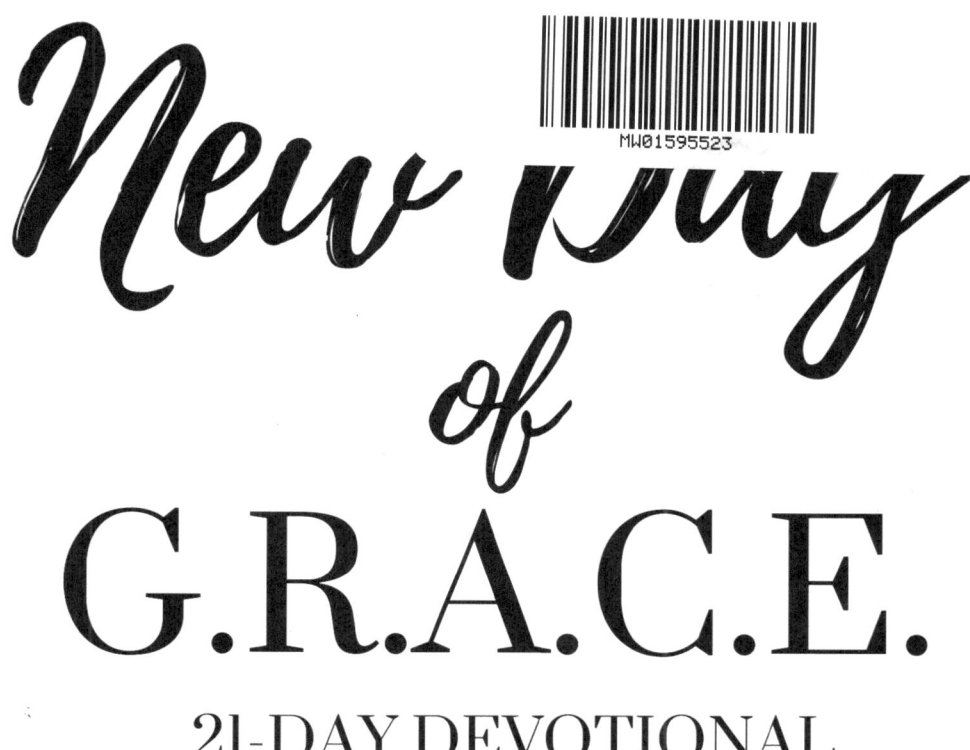

New Day of
G.R.A.C.E.

2l-DAY DEVOTIONAL

1/29/2024

Dawn Charleston-Green, Author

INTRODUCING CONTRIBUTORS
Leon J. Green, Jr. - Anna M. Jackson - Gamellia Davis -
Ashley Thomas - Rudolph A. Valentine, III

1/20/2024

ISBN: 979-8-9880305-0-8 (Paperback)
       979-8-9880305-3-9 (eBook)

Printed in the United States of America.

First printing, 2023.

Dawn of a New Day 365, LLC
P.O. BOX 384
Grovetown, Ga 30813
www.dawnofanewday365.com

Dedication

I dedicate this devotion to everyone who has had to experience the gripping effect of starting over due to life's losses, transitions, failures, or disappointments.
Be encouraged that no matter what it is or may have been. . . it is a part of God's perfect will and plan for your life.
He wastes nothing.

Table of Contents

Week 3

Foreword

Life can be scary. It can even hurt sometimes. Our past and even our present can scar us. Think about losing a loved one or a close friend, or receiving an uncomfortable diagnosis that will require life-long treatment. Even the "close calls" leave a mark.

It is not always the end result of the circumstances of situations that hurt the most. Sometimes the "waiting" is just as painful. Waiting on that test result, after having been hit with one setback after another can be devastating. Or maybe awaiting trial for a false accusation. The enemy is going to throw all that he can to try to distract and discourage us. The Bible tells us that Satan has come to steal, kill and destroy (John 10:10) and describes him as the accuser of our brethren (Revelation 12:10).

So what happens when we feel like all is lost?... When we feel like we have been burnt by our past or present circumstances, we remind ourselves of God's word. Isaiah 61:3 (NIV) says:

> *"and provide for those who grieve in Zion-*
> *to bestow on them a crown of beauty instead of ashes,*
> *the oil of joy instead of mourning, and a garment of praise*
> *instead of the spirit of despair.*
> *They will be called oaks of righteousness,*
> *a planting of the Lord for the display of his splendor."*

In this 21-day devotional, Dawn Charleston-Green brings women from all walks of life together for one purpose - to glorify God and remind us of the beauty for ashes that come through knowing and understanding His Grace.

During this journey, you are going to experience God's glory and recognize His grace like never before! Ever since I met Dawn, over 2 or 3 years ago, that has been her focus. Every time I talk to her, still to this day, she reminds me what the Word says!

I remember when she accepted the invitation to my "Lift a Sister Up Roundtable Talk." That was my first time hosting anything. I had NO IDEA what I was doing! I laugh because I remember it like it was yesterday. Dawn was my guest, yet she stepped in and helped me just when I needed it; AND... she did it with such poise and GRACE. And, we were not even as close as we are now. What Dawn did for me in that moment is what we need; to remember God's grace for us and remember to GIVE grace to others.

We should all surround ourselves with praying friends that will remind us that no matter what we may be facing, and no matter what it looks like, GOD IS NEAR! All of the hurt and pain will not last as long as we think, and we will be fulfilled with God's promise!

So, as Dawn ushers you through this devotional, be on the lookout for the good! It is coming! As you begin to be encouraged and testify of God's grace toward you, you may notice that your beauty for ashes may look different from others around you. Remember, only God knows what He has in store for you. But that's just it: GOD KNOWS. Trust him, surrender all to Him, and let Him use you and mold you in EVERY way! Whatever comes from it, with God leading... will be BEAUTIFUL, because of His GRACE.

Ashley Thomas
Christian Author, Entrepreneur, and Minister
ThaVineRevelations

BEAUTIFUL THINGS

are in store for

YOU

...even though the process may seem
ugly and uncomfortable

NEW DAY OF G.R.A.C.E.

Preface

Whoever thought that the 4-letter word I almost hated as a child...would end up being my platform?

Hello! If you're not already familiar with me, my name is Dawn Charleston-Green, award-winning author of the 5-Day Morning C.O.F.F.E.E. Devotional and the children's book, Heeeyy Dandelion. I am also the founder and creator of the blog and platform Dawn of a New Day 365.

DND365 is a movement for women journeying through everyday life (the good, bad, ugly, and unexpected); overcoming through TRUTH and TRANSPARENCY in a way that leads to TRANSFORMATION.

Whew! That's a mouthful, isn't it? But, does that sound like something you're interested in being a part of? I hope you said, "Yes;" because if so, you're in the right place.

So, let me give you a little bit of background about me, my name, and why I wrote the 21-day devotion, New Day of G.R.A.C.E.

The name. Again, it's Dawn (like the morning), Charleston (like the city), and Green (just like the color); and yes, I play off my name all the time, but it wasn't always that way.

What's In A Name?

Dawn. D-A-W-N. Four letters. One syllable.

As a child, I disliked my name. I won't say that I hated it...but I wasn't particularly fond of it AT ALL. I knew that it was different...but why was it different? And better yet, why was it so short? Why Dawn?

Apparently, my mom wanted my name to be different from the other little girls who looked like me, who at the time were endearingly named Tameka, LaShonda, LaTasha, and Keisha. And as popular, common, and overused as those names were in the 1970s, I sure wished I was in that number. Heck! Even the girls who didn't look like me were named Heather, Stephanie, Tiffany, and Jennifer.

I thought to myself "Mom!!! What were you thinking?!?!?! Dawn!? Really!? Dawn?!?"

One day, however, my grandmother explained something to me about my name that took me to become an adult to comprehend; explaining that one day I would not only understand the meaning of my name but I would also walk into its calling. "It's calling?!" What did that mean?

Grandmomma expounded by saying my name meant light and that part of my purpose was to bring light to people; especially those in places of darkness. Honestly, I had no clue what that meant. In fact, I was a little intimidated by the thought. It sounded like a lot of responsibility. Furthermore, what I didn't foresee was that in learning or finding that purpose, my "dawn" wouldn't be revealed until I experienced a definitive season of darkness.

Dusk Till Dawn

Have you ever heard the saying, "It's always darkest just before dawn"? Well, it is true both in thought and theory. The phrase "from dusk till dawn" refers to the period of time between sunset and sunrise when the sun is below the horizon. I don't know about you, but I have had some periods in my life when the light I carry was buried beneath the surface. Not only was it unable to be seen by others, but barely visible to me. Yes. This Dawn has experienced her share of darkness.

Let me share a little background. About 4 years ago, at the age of 45, I had to relinquish some things I had become accustomed to; things that had been a part of my identity as a person, in my career, and in my family. Some of these things were previous victories and accomplishments I associated with my success.

Can you imagine doing this at 45? I had to completely start over. Reinvent myself. But guess what I learned? I wasn't reinventing myself. I was walking into the new and intentional season God had planned for me from the very beginning.

During this perceived season of darkness, what I learned was . . . though it was a new place for me, God had strategically orchestrated it with me in mind when He "invented me" in my mother's womb. Yes, close to 50 years ago, God knew that I would be a wife, mother, author, speaker. . . and He even knew that I would find myself in darkness.

Though being in that place caught ME completely off guard, who I am today, and who I am becoming, is not now, nor was it ever, a surprise to God. He keeps commanding me to "BE STRONG, AND OF GOOD COURAGE!"

What I will say is that the journey to getting here wasn't straight according to human standards. However, I know now more than ever that it led me straight to God. . . for Him to get the glory.

To be clear, though I may sound optimistic, know that this was not an easy path by any means. No. This road of life has definitely been a crooked one. In fact, it almost felt like I was pushed from a cliff. Yet, I hold to the expression that says,

"When God pushes you to the edge of difficulty,
TRUST HIM FULLY.
Either two things will happen.
He will catch you when you fall,
or He will teach you to fly."
~Unknown~

In my case, I think He did both.

Same Feeling Different Purpose

I've shared this before, but during times when I felt life had buried me, I learned that I was actually being planted. Or, in times when I felt like I was being cut, I learned I was instead being pruned. These things look and feel the same but serve different purposes.

When something is buried it's usually because it's dead. It has no more life. Dead things decay never to come back, and take on the likeness of what has covered it. But, when something has been planted, after going through a process in darkness. . . it rises to the surface bringing forth more life than it went down with.

Similarly, branches that are cut from a tree are then thrown into a wood chipper or into a fire and destroyed. Branches that are pruned, however, are done so with the intent that what once held them will yield a greater harvest than it did in the previous season.

Friend, regardless of what has happened to me, I'm rising from the ground from which I was planted; bearing the scars from my pruning. But this dirt on my face and my scars tell a testimony, and I will tell the truth of their stories if it means helping another woman emerge into seeing the grace given to her for her New Day.

All Things Are New

Through this 21-day devotion, my hope is to help you embrace the place you're in or the places God has allowed you to be. Know that it is not by chance. It is on purpose. And what's best. . . you're going to survive and be a better, stronger, and wiser version of yourself because of it. God wastes nothing.

Despite whatever setback, loss, or disappointment you previously encountered, it's time for you to reset your goals and purpose. Know that God is not done with you yet. Regardless of what your earthly name might be, know that God calls you daughter and He loves you. The light that is in you will rise above the surface and shine bright for yourself and others. And everything that may have held you bound in your past will be used to continue to make you beautiful.

I celebrate your growth in advance, and I am pleased that you've chosen to take your journey into discovering your NEW DAY.

GOD IS IN THE MIDST OF HER, SHE SHALL NOT BE MOVED; GOD SHALL HELP HER, JUST AT THE BREAK OF DAWN.

~PSALM 46:5~

A New Day of G.R.A.C.E.

Introduction

Well, Friend, know that this devotional is beginning exactly where the 5-Day Morning C.O.F.F.E.E. Devotion ended. Now, I hope you were able to dive into that one too, and learn more about God's character; understanding that you don't have to be what He promises to be for you – LOVE, JOY, STRENGTH, PEACE, & SUSTAINMENT. But if not, it's no problem. A New Day of G.R.A.C.E is an absolutely perfect place to START, RE-START, RESET, or REINFORCE your faith journey.

As I mentioned, the 5-Day Morning C.O.F.F.E.E. Devotion ended with a reminder of Lamentations 3:22-23 (KJV) which says,

> "It is [because] of the Lord's MERCIES
> that we are not consumed,
> because his COMPASSIONS fail not.
> They are NEW EVERY MORNING:
> Great is thy FAITHFULNESS.

Isn't it wonderful to be reminded that God's mercies are new for everyone each and every day? So, we can wake up each morning expecting God to do something great.

Not only can we expect Him to provide for our basic needs, but we can also have hope that He is able to do NEW THINGS that we have never seen before. Yes! God's new mercies for us mean that He will have compassion and forgiveness toward us despite where we might find ourselves.

I've said it before. Fortunately, God doesn't pack our baggage from yesterday and bring it to us today, consuming us with our past, and neither should we.

So then, we must let go of unforgiveness, past mistakes, past hurts, regrets, and disappointments. I know that may be hard, but when we look for God even in unexpected circumstances in life, He'll show up in ways we've never imagined. He's faithful like that. And each day He gives us a New Day of GRACE.

Now, Ephesians 2:8-10 (NIV) teaches us,

> "For it is by God's GRACE that you have been saved
> through faith. It is not the result of your own efforts,
> but God's gift, so that no one can boast about it.
> God has made us what we are,
> and in our union with Christ Jesus
> he has created us for a life of [good works],
> which he has already prepared for us to do."

Listen. I don't know how to explain it any better than that. So, I'll just reiterate it for effect. Follow me here. . .

It's because of God's GRACE – his unmerited divine favor given to us for RE-generation and cleansing from our troubles that saves us. It's not because of anything we did with our own abilities, but God's GRACE . . . IS His gift to us. And when He renders His gift of grace, we'll know it and know that whatever He has provided us we could have never done on our own. We don't have the strength or the natural proclivity to even be that gracious to ourselves.

In addition, God made us EXACTLY who we are and how we are on purpose; and He unified us with His son, Jesus Christ, so that we might carry out the good deeds we were created to do...that He purposed within us from the very beginning.

Have you heard the saying, "If not for the GRACE of God...?" That's a true statement. Regardless of where you may be today, or what led you to this devotion, "if not for the GRACE of God," you wouldn't be here. No matter how good your life is, or how uncertain or complicated it might be at this very moment...if God's grace and mercy weren't upon your life EACH DAY, you wouldn't even have the wherewithal to do even the simplest of things. Not anything.

No matter how minimal or difficult, we can do nothing unless God allows it to happen in and through us. No life, health, strength, activities, successes .. Nothing.

My Friend, God is keeping you and has kept you up until this very point. Give Him glory!

Though this day, or the days before this one, may not have been perfect, it's a NEW DAY. It is a day you've never seen before. One you will never see again. So, consider yourself CHOSEN; because you were.

Listen! You may have heard me say this before, but I'll say it again . . .Not everyone saw this day or had an opportunity for a new season, but you do. God wastes nothing, and neither should you.

On this day, God offers and will provide for you His LOVE, JOY, and His STRENGTH. Not only that, but He also offers you His compassion and favor – His MERCY and His GRACE.

So, dear friend, release anything (mentally, emotionally, or spiritually) that would keep you from walking into this day able to receive all God has in store for you; so that you can be your best self - the best you that He created you for.

WHAT TO EXPECT

As you go through this devotional journey, you will receive a practical lesson each day coupled with scripture and insight to help provide perspective and encouragement. The hope is that you will then reflect upon what you've gathered and apply it to your own faith journey.

Most of the lessons, God has allowed me over the last two years to construct. However, for this devotional, I solicited the assistance of other faith influencers - Elder Leon J. Green, Jr. (12), Pastor Anna M. Jackson (16), Minister Gamellia F. Davis (17), Minister Ashley J. Smith (7), and Rudolph Valentine, III (15). The numbers behind their names represent the corresponding days of their contributions. I pray that you witness how each of the lessons, regardless of the author, is ordained by God to strengthen your faith.

GRACE

As I'm sure you've noticed, the word GRACE is poured throughout the reading. We'll be using the acronym G.R.A.C.E. throughout this devotion. As you go through each lesson, you'll complete your daily reflections and prayer by using the acronym. In addition, each lesson concludes with the "Thought-for-Today" (TFT). Space is also provided for you to ponder on these reflections as well.

For a better explanation, observe the next page.

G - Give GRATITUDE for what God's provided, and for what and/or who you're THANKFUL for in your life.

R - REPENT of anything that you did in ignorance or selfishness; anything that was in poor taste that didn't represent the spirit of God and His nature in your life. Those things that hinder you from being the best person you can be to fulfill the divine purpose God has for you. Acknowledge and turn from those things.

A - ASSESS where you are today and what is helping you or hindering you in moving forward. Maybe there are some things that you do well. Ask God for more strength and discipline to keep doing them. Likewise, if there are habits or patterns of thinking that keep you stuck, ask God for strength and discipline, as well as deliverance, to help you break those tendencies.

C - Take time to COMMUNE (be with) and COMMUNICATE (talk about) what your needs are to God. Talk to Him in an intimate way, like He knows your exact feelings and desires. Because guess what?! He does. He wants to fulfill His purpose in you; so, the more you talk to Him, the better you'll be able to hear Him talking back to you, giving you the answers you need. Understand this. He knows you, but He always wants to further cultivate the relationship; so, don't hold back.

E - Once you've assessed where you are and talked with God, now you'll need a plan of execution. How will you EXECUTE what it is that you need to do? You must ask yourself what you need to do personally, and then what God is requiring of you. These two things will have to work in tandem (side-by-side) in order for you to not only come into who you want to be in your new season but also who God has called you to be.

New Day of

of

G.R.A.C.E.

21-DAY DEVOTIONAL

TODAY

Listen. If God woke you up today, know that you don't have to be stuck in anything from yesterday. That's not what He intended. A new day is exactly what it is...NEW - never seen before or existing. When we think of it this way, we would actually be giving our days a disservice to weigh them down with yesterday's issues. Let's begin to approach each day with vibrancy and a new mindset.

It's been said that the essence of stupidity is doing the same thing repeatedly and expecting a new outcome. I'm by no means calling you stupid, but I'll just gently say...If you know that you've been doing some things that don't benefit you or serve you well...let's try to switch it up a little.

Research says it takes 21 days to develop a habit – good or bad. That's why this is a 21-day devotion. I want you to develop the habit of expecting something new from God every day, and approaching each day that you've been given with the expectation that something great is possible.

Remember, you've been given a gift by God of both favor and compassion. Hopefully, that will allow you to approach each day with freedom and not worry. Freedom of knowing that God IS who He is; reassuring you that you are connected to everything you need to become who you're supposed to be.

I truly believe there's something new on the horizon; the likes which we have never seen before. Whatever it is, though, will offer us a HOPE and FUTURE just as God's word said it would in Jeremiah 29:11. I believe this is the Dawn of YOUR New Day. Let it mark the beginning of your "day one" and not just "one day". TODAY, rejoice and be thankful for God's New Day of G.R.A.CE. ~Dawn

"
Wherever life
plants you,
Bloom
with
Grace.
"

Day One

Dawn of a New Day

God is in the midst of her,
she shall not be moved;
he shall help her,
just at the break of dawn.
~Psalm 46:5 (NKJV)~

For obvious reasons, today's scripture is one of my favorites. Not just because my name is in it, but rather, because it tells of God's ability to protect us during the time of storm, and to bring change to our situation just in the nick of time.

Listen. I know when we're in the thick of uncertain circumstances, it seems like it's impossible for relief to come and save us. But, we can be reassured that help is on the way. I think it would help us, however, to consider timing in a better way, by also taking conditions into consideration. What are the conditions affecting the timing of our relief?

Now, understand. . . I am a military veteran; so I use some of those experiences to help me process other situations. With any tactical mission that we approached, we always had to conduct a risk assessment. Risk assessments are necessary to determine the overall probability of hazards and other factors that could potentially affect the success of the mission. Though the mission would need to be completed, successful completion was contingent on the presence or absence of certain conditions.

An example that may be more relatable might be thinking of victims caught in a natural disaster. They need to be rescued as soon as possible, but the overall conditions must be considered so that those providing the rescue won't be harmed in the process. Now, let's just be clear. We know that there are no conditions that could exist that can restrict God's ability to save us. However, considering natural things, on a rescue mission, what is the most advantageous route that can be taken to ensure not only safety, but also preservation of life? It's usually not a direct route, and it may take some time and even several attempts. But once the rescue is made, the rescuers will go back and assess their process, while those rescued will take away both gratitude, as well as lessons learned.

Most likely, though, both will consider future storms from a different vantage point. Their experiences will help them critically analyze factors that will help ensure safety. And, what can probably be certain is neither will take the chance of being unprepared in the likelihood of another storm.

If we're honest, sometimes life seems like a natural disaster; and we're just waiting for a rescue. Don't worry. Help is coming. But ask yourself these questions:
- What are the conditions that surround you that could be hindering your rescue?
- What are the lessons you've learned previously that could ensure your safety?
- Are there some decisions that you've made negligently or out of ignorance that may have caused you to be in this place?

Let me encourage you to stand firm in your faith and your confidence in who God is. He is a well-qualified rescuer who can see you through whatever you may face. But as you sit in the mental basement listening to the winds of your situation, or stand on the mental rooftop surrounded by water; look up and then listen closely. There is a voice saying, "Come to me. Give me your hand. Don't worry. You won't fall. You're safe with me."

Grab on and hold on real tight. Your rescuer will not only take you to safety, but He'll stay with you and strengthen you. You're going to be okay. Surprisingly, even after all of this. . . What seemed like it was the end isn't . . . The sun will shine tomorrow. "Just at the break of DAWN."

––––––––––––––––––––

TFT: How does knowing God is your rescuer help you to understand where you are currently in your life and what is possible?

My thoughts for today...

G.R.A.C.E.

Use the acronym G.R.A.C.E to reflect on today's lesson.

G. What are you most grateful for today?
_____
_____
_____

R. As you reflect back on today's lesson, what remains on your mind and why?
_____
_____

A. What could YOU have done differently? What would need to change in order to get better results?
_____
_____

C. Commune - This is your time to pray and communicate with God. You can write it or say it aloud; but at least write down key points, so you can keep a record of your conversation and concern for God.
_____
_____

E. Based on today's lesson what action do you need to take?
_____
_____

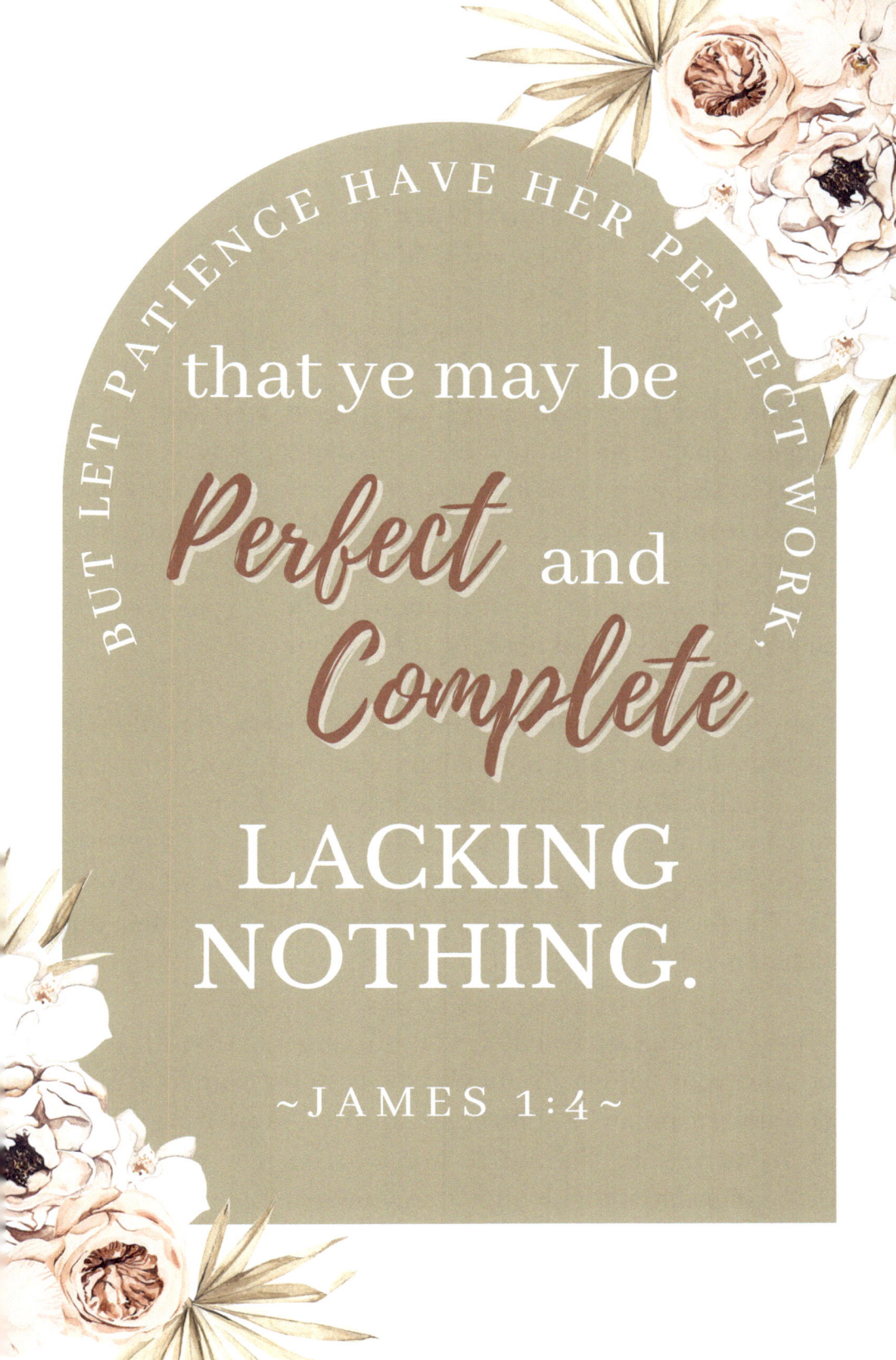

BUT LET PATIENCE HAVE HER PERFECT WORK,

that ye may be

Perfect and

Complete

LACKING
NOTHING.

~JAMES 1:4~

Day Two

Get Your Heart Checked

My flesh and my heart faileth:
but God is the strength of my heart,
and my portion forever.
~Psalm 73:26 (KJV)~

A little over two years ago, I was faced with one of the biggest challenges of my life – giving up my career to address some family concerns. Even as tired as I may have gotten from performing every day, I'll admit, I wouldn't have left my job on my own without a clear plan of action. Yet there I was, needing to transition at the age of 45 for a reason that really had nothing to do with me.

Come to think of it, about 10 years prior to this, I had faced a similar situation with my military career. I chose to resign my commission as an Army Officer to save my marriage. And I will be honest, FOR YEARS I was unsure if I made the right decision. Giving up everything you've worked so hard for, for the sake of someone else, seems a bit unfair and unbalanced.

When circumstances catch you off guard and seem to be beyond your control, or they're the result of someone else's decision or behavior, bitterness and resentment can easily begin to set in. They can begin to change your whole demeanor and outlook on not only people; but also, on how you view your life. When this happens those inner emotions begin to attack you from the inside like a cancer. They become debilitating. Pretty soon those emotions begin to negatively affect your relationships and cripple how or whether you move forward in your purpose.

In my experience, even though I had a time when I allowed myself to feel those emotions of frustration and disappointment, I knew within myself that I was a child of the King. And when you are a child of the King, your outcome has favor attached to it. I knew that God had a plan and purpose for me; and that He hadn't brought me that far in life – in my marriage, career, or as a person – to leave me in that place. So, I trusted that His thoughts were better than my thoughts and His plan was better than my plan.

What I knew most of all was that allowing myself to sit in bitterness and self-pity would only hinder me and my purpose and no one else's.

So, I asked God to "check" me (in both senses of the word). I wanted God to check me and put me in my place from feeling like I was beyond going through trials and testing. And, I wanted God to perform an examination of my heart and mind.

What was it in me that was affecting my thought process? What was it in me that was holding grudges and resentment? What I knew for certain was that nothing could happen that God did not allow. So, I needed to stop giving those whom I felt wronged me or disregarded me power and authority. God was always in control, PERIOD!

If we are to fulfill our purpose and calling, our hearts and minds have to be right toward God and His people. There are going to be some things that He calls us to that will involve not just us, but other relationships we're in. Yes, there is a life that we have to live as individuals, but some of the work that must be done in the earth will require that we operate in tandem with other people; so we must pray and ask God to give us a right heart towards them.

Now, because people aren't perfect beings, there are going to be times when they say and do things we don't approve of, agree with, or like; but that doesn't change the fact that they're made in God's image. Therefore, the same grace that is rendered to us, we must render to them. When we find ourselves in difficult circumstances with people, we should refer to the latter part of the scripture text found in Psalm 51:12 which says,

> "*Restore to me the joy of Your salvation,*
> *And uphold me by Your generous Spirit.*"

Through everything we face, good or bad, we have to remember who we are and whose we are. We have salvation through Christ Jesus, regardless of our circumstances. That fact alone makes everything else pale in comparison. But, I get it. Sometimes life gets hard and seems unfair. However, the scripture here is telling us that our joy can be RESTORED. Let's use David's example here and just ask. We can ask God to uphold us through His spirit working through us. Because let's face it, unless we are willing to allow God's spirit to work through us, we won't be able to navigate through life alone, and certainly not with others.

In case you're wondering, yes, the challenges and sacrifices I had to make were worth it. In fact, looking back, if those circumstances wouldn't have arisen, I probably wouldn't be writing this devotion . . . trying to help others to keep the faith and understand how to better navigate through setbacks--whether in marriage, career, parenting, or just life.

So, please be encouraged; no matter what challenges you face or have faced, know that God's plan for you is perfect. Your joy can be restored.

I pray that God gives you a newly created clean heart so that you can fulfill His calling, whether alone or with others. No matter what today's results show, know that trusting God is ALWAYS worth it!

TFT: What does God see when He's checking your heart? Is your heart right with yourself and others?

My thoughts for today...

_____

_____

_____

_____

_____

_____

_____

_____

_____

_____

_____

_____

_____

_____

_____

_____

_____

_____

_____

_____

_____

_____

_____

Conclude with G.R.A.C.E.

G.R.A.C.E.

Use the acronym G.R.A.C.E to reflect on today's lesson.

G. What are you most grateful for today?

_____
_____
_____

R. As you reflect back on today's lesson, what remains on your mind and why?

_____
_____

A. What could YOU have done differently? What would need to change in order to get better results?

_____
_____

C. Commune - This is your time to pray and communicate with God. You can write it or say it aloud; but at least write down key points, so you can keep a record of your conversation and concern for God.

_____
_____

E. Based on today's lesson what action do you need to take?

_____
_____

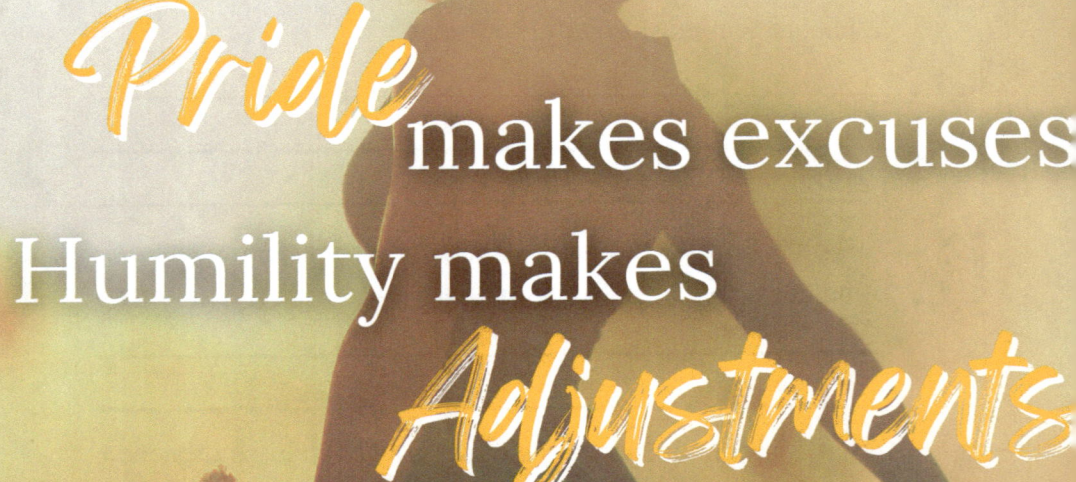

Pride makes excuses
Humility makes
Adjustments

dawn

NEW DAY OF G.R.A.C.E.

Day Three

God is Good!

For the LORD is good;
his mercy is everlasting;
And his truth endureth to all generations.
~Psalm 100:5 (KJV)~

I can recall one spring break while my son was in college. We had been preparing for him to take the long drive from Louisiana to visit us back in Georgia. We were all super excited; because with my son being a student-athlete, he didn't get a chance to visit home often during the regular school year.

It was the day my son was to travel home. He had his oil changed, his tire pressure checked, and had just picked up a fellow schoolmate (also from Georgia) to ride along with him. They were about forty-five minutes into their trip when they realized the car wasn't running well. When my son called, he described that his car was vibrating. Not being familiar enough with cars, I just asked him if the car seemed undrivable. At least if it were drivable, he could make it home so that we (my husband and I) could have the car completely serviced. It's hard making those types of decisions when your child is so far from home. While he was visiting, we could take care of what needed to be done, so we could at least have peace of mind on his return.

After assessing the situation as much as he could, my son thought he was okay to drive; so he continued. A short while later, however, his tire was flat. Unfortunately, by this time, he was in an area where no services were available. So, it was time for roadside assistance.

When the tow truck arrived, the driver explained that the issue seemed to be greater than just a flat tire (which he could have fixed on the spot), so he suggested that my son seek a licensed mechanic. The only problem was, they would have to travel all the way back to the last major city in order to be helped, and that would be outside of the coverage area for towing. Realizing, fortunately, that these two were novices to car repair, the driver agreed he would take them where they needed to go at no additional cost.

Still, imagine my disappointment and feelings of helplessness when I got the word. I was so excited to have my son come home, but at this point, they were making no forward progress toward Georgia. And worse, there was nothing I could really do about it.

They were heading back to Monroe, LA. However, this also meant, they were close enough to an uncle we have who worked in the car industry for years. Surely he could suggest a mechanic who might be able to take a look at my son's car and tell us what was wrong.

Even though I hadn't spoken to Uncle Jay in quite some time, when I called, he immediately said, "Have the driver bring them straight here. I'll take care of it from there and let you know what you're looking at."

Quite a bit of time passed and I hadn't heard from anyone. No news is good news, they say, but it never feels like that when you're waiting. When I finally got someone on the phone, it was my aunt. She shared that my son and Uncle Jay had left for the mechanic shop my uncle frequently used and were getting the car fixed.

"Fixed?!" I thought. This should be a good thing, right? But, it still made me a little worried because I would have preferred to talk about the diagnosis and the cost associated with it before a decision was made. I didn't want to commit to something I couldn't afford.

When I finally got through to Uncle Jay, surprisingly, he was in very good spirits. He didn't sound at all like someone who had been unexpectedly inconvenienced on a Saturday afternoon. He immediately began to share that what was wrong with my son's car had to be handled right away. Otherwise, my son wouldn't be able to safely drive the car anywhere, longless Georgia, without a chance of incident.

He further shared, "These young people today just drive these cars; they have no idea how to maintain them." I agreed but was a little embarrassed that we hadn't done more to prepare my son for times like this. Uncle Jay continued, "My grandkids are the same way, but at least we're blessed to be in a position to help them." Again I agreed.

I asked, "Uncle Jay, how much will it cost and how do I take care of the payment?" He calmly expressed, "I've already taken care of the cost, and Tre and I have already bought a new tire. He's good to go!"

Shocked, I replied, "You did?!"

"Yes! I wasn't gonna have my nephew this far away from home and not be able to be safe."

Tears welled in my eyes. Uncle Jay didn't just act as an uncle in that moment, he stepped in as a father for a son that needed it.

"Thank you so much, Uncle Jay. How do I pay you?" I asked. He replied, " You don't have to worry about it right now, because I know you are thinking about other things, like just getting your baby home. Call your aunt later and y'all can work out the details."

Even though Uncle Jay told me I could wait to repay him, I went ahead and took care of it immediately. When someone is that gracious to you at a moment's notice, you just want to make sure your gratitude is evident.

In retrospect, this experience was God reminding me how good He is. My son and his schoolmate could have broken down anywhere along the 10-hour journey; yet, they broke down just in reach of Uncle Jay, and he knew exactly how to handle it. He was God's ambassador for us. And even though my son didn't know Uncle Jay as well as I had known him as a child, his kindness and commitment to him was a sign of God's truth enduring to all generations.

Sometimes we're just living our lives with no idea how to maintain them from day to day; much less with a proper perspective of the future. Fortunately, God steps in and takes care of even that which we don't know needs to be taken care of.

When we are in distress, know that regardless of how distant we might feel from God, we are still within reach; and He knows exactly what to do and whom He needs to connect us to in order that His blessings might be bestowed upon us. Our inconveniences don't inconvenience God. He'll be there at a moment's notice. We must be grateful for his graciousness to show us mercy despite not always being in relationship with Him the way we should.

Sometimes we're disappointed because of circumstances that happen beyond our control. And, we may even feel that rather than going forward in life, we're going backwards. We may try to assess our situations, like my son did, and think that we are okay to continue; but sometimes we actually need to stay in place and get proper instruction before going forward. Staying in place might be just what is needed for our growth and safety.

God is never going to leave us or forsake us. He'll always step in as a Father should.

Know this, my son (now two years post college graduation) never visits Monroe, LA now without giving a shout-out to Uncle Jay. He is eternally grateful for his kindness towards him. That's the same way we should be towards God.

We should never forget His kindness towards us; knowing that we could never repay him for what He's done. Our only repayment can be our immediate praise and gratitude.

Why did I share this story? Because I wanted to give you encouragement today whether you are a parent, or whether you are someone still connected to the benefits of a parent or caregiver...or maybe you're just singularly you. Regardless, know that you don't have to worry. You are covered. God is good. His mercy still endures to bless us, our children, our children's children, and their children.

Trust God, his plan, and his process. The same God who has been faithful in the past will remain faithful to those He loves. Aren't you glad you're in the family?

———————————

TFT: How can God's goodness be seen in your life Currently?

My thoughts for today...

_____

_____

_____

_____

_____

_____

_____

_____

_____

_____

_____

_____

_____

_____

_____

_____

_____

_____

_____

_____

_____

_____

_____

_____

Conclude with G.R.A.C.E.

G.R.A.C.E.

Use the acronym G.R.A.C.E to reflect on today's lesson.

G. What are you most grateful for today?

_____

_____

_____

R. As you reflect back on today's lesson, what remains on your mind and why?

_____

_____

A. What could YOU have done differently? What would need to change in order to get better results?

_____

_____

C. Commune - This is your time to pray and communicate with God. You can write it or say it aloud; but at least write down key points, so you can keep a record of your conversation and concern for God.

_____

_____

E. Based on today's lesson what action do you need to take?

_____

_____

Be hopeful for the NEW THING God is doing. Even though you can't see it now, BELIEVE that it's going to be GREATER than anything you've already seen.

dawn

NEW DAY OF G.R.A.C.E.

Day Four

Don't Be Afraid of the Dark

1 In the beginning God created the heaven and the earth.
2 And the earth was without form, and void;
and darkness was upon the face of the deep.
And the Spirit of God moved upon the face of the waters.
3 And God said, Let there be light: and there was light.
4 And God saw the light, that it was good:
and God divided the light from the darkness.
5 And God called the light Day, and the darkness he called Night.
And the evening and the morning were the first day.
~Genesis 1:1-5 (KJV)~

This, as many know, is the very first scripture in the Bible; and I actually find it to be one of the most encouraging when it comes to understanding creation and/or starting over.

When something is starting out, there is nothingness present. Likewise, typically when we're starting over, we feel a void or an emptiness, or that we're in a place of darkness. Generally, we also feel isolated and alone.

What Genesis 1:1 says to me is that this is an environment that God is familiar with.

In verse 2 it specifically says that the earth was without form and void - a place or condition of familiarity to some when life seems uncertain; especially during times of difficult decisions, major transitions, or loss.

The verse then goes on to describe the deepest parts of the earth as being blanketed with darkness. I don't know about anyone else, but I have had moments in my life – in my marriage, career, while parenting, after multiple miscarriages, and difficulties in relationships – that took me to the depths of what seemed to be a very dark place. In fact, this place seemed so dark at times that the evidence of even the slightest glimpse of light seemed unlikely.

Verse 2 concludes, however, by saying, "And the Spirit of God moved upon the face of the waters."

Wait! So, it was dark. . . and God was moving there?

Yep!

Do you know why?

Because He was creating it.

The scripture began by informing us that "In the beginning, God created the heavens and the earth. AND...

The "AND" reveals to us that the creation and the darkness were happening in tandem (together/at the same time). So, even in the darkness, God's presence was always there. However, the presence of darkness didn't hinder God from creating. No, on the contrary, it was actually in the darkness that God spoke, "Let there be light" and light appeared. Likewise, we should remember, our dark circumstances don't stop God from creating something new in us (or for us) that has never been seen before.

No matter how dark your situation may seem, be assured that God is moving. Though it might cause you alarm, your darkness doesn't frighten God. But the question I ask is this. In your darkness, what are you speaking? Are you speaking to your situation to let there be light so that you can see and have better clarity for what is ahead? Are you asking God to give you something new and fresh that will help you fulfill the purpose He has ordained for you in the earth?

The passage of scripture goes on to tell us that God saw that the light was good. It was good for Him and it's good for you, and He knows that. Know that God is capable of dividing your light from your darkness. Likewise, also know that while you might be in your dark place God is creating something new and better for you.

Be encouraged and think of this scripture whenever you're doubtful that there are no better days ahead. Better days are possible and coming. Just remember, in the scripture, "the evening and the morning were the first day," which then reminds us that the darkness came first.

Don't despise your darkness or be afraid of it. God is with you and for you. Claim today as the first day of your new beginning.

———————————

TFT: Are you now, or have you ever been, in a dark place? What was/is your response or concern?

My thoughts for today...

_____

_____

_____

_____

_____

_____

_____

_____

_____

_____

_____

_____

_____

_____

_____

_____

_____

_____

_____

_____

_____

_____

_____

_____

Conclude with G.R.A.C.E.

G.R.A.C.E.

Use the acronym G.R.A.C.E to reflect on today's lesson.

G. What are you most grateful for today?
_____
_____
_____

R. As you reflect back on today's lesson, what remains on your mind and why?
_____
_____

A. What could YOU have done differently? What would need to change in order to get better results?
_____
_____

C. Commune - This is your time to pray and communicate with God. You can write it or say it aloud; but at least write down key points, so you can keep a record of your conversation and concern for God.
_____
_____

E. Based on today's lesson what action do you need to take?
_____
_____

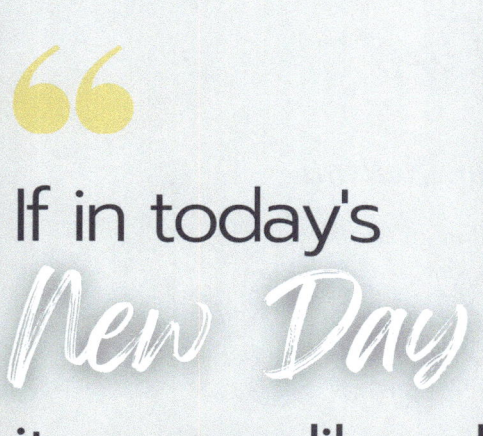

If in today's *New Day* it seems like all that surrounds you looks *Dark*; remember… it's always darkest just before *Dawn*

Day Five

You're in a New Season

Therefore if any man be in Christ,
he is a new creature:
old things are passed away;
behold, all things are become new.
~2 Corinthians 5:17 (KJV)~

As you take this journey into embracing newness, regard this as a newness of seasons. I suggest that you regard it as a newness of seasons because I believe becoming new is an ever-evolving process. We are constantly being made over into better versions of ourselves for our purpose in the next season.

Yes, I do believe that we all have an overarching purpose in life, but along the way of getting to that place, there are other seasons of purpose that must take place in between. Each day that you wake up and you believe that God is who He is, and that He is who He is in you, you must believe that you are new. God himself is a creator. Better put, He's THE CREATOR.

It's us who get caught up in dates, planners, calendars, and timelines. We make resolutions and plans to begin a new task or goal. Can I assure you of something? God is not limited to the calendar. He does not need to wait for our birthdays or Christmas to gift us anything. Nor does He have to wait until the New Year to begin a new work in us. In fact, the scripture tells us in Philippians 1:6 that

> . . . *"being confident of this very thing,*
> *that He who hath begun a good work in you will perform it*
> *until the Day of Jesus Christ."*

You may feel you're just starting on your journey or reclaiming one; but be confident that God ALREADY began a GOOD WORK in you, and He will perform (carry out, accomplish, or fulfill) bringing forth the purpose He put in you until Jesus comes. So just know, new possibilities are ahead and available to you. . . TODAY.

When we consider new things that are ahead and available to us, we must be willing to set aside anything that would hinder us from going forward in our newness. Oldness, staleness, old trophies . . . those things not only keep us from going into our new place; but also, from embracing or appreciating our newness as we should.

So again, consider that newness comes to us each season. Think for a moment. There is no season that we experience in the natural . . . that doesn't serve a purpose. Likewise, you must believe that there is no season in the spiritual that doesn't also serve a purpose.

I think of it this way. . .If the physical seasons didn't serve a purpose, we could probably expect that it would be spring and summer all year long. But that CAN'T happen, because God created everything to have a process and a cycle of life, regeneration, and death.

As I'm writing this devotion, summer is preparing to end. In the natural sense, everything has reached full maturity, richness, and growth. The harvest that was planted has grown. But guess what? As this season ends, all that has grown must be plucked up; and then the ground turned over on any seed that remains.

Following the summer comes fall. Things in nature will begin to change their color and begin to fall away. But do you know something? That which gave life to what will fall away isn't dead. When the leaves fall from the tree, the tree isn't dead; the roots simply draw back their nutrients in order to preserve life under the surface. By doing so, the tree will have less to contend with during the winds and rains that will come with winter.

When winter comes, some things will appear frozen in time. They will lie in rest during inclement weather until the season passes. When it warms up again, they'll come back.

What happens next? Spring.

The March winds come and blow away everything that has been lying dormant, and the wind makes space for the rain – the "April showers" to help give new life to the seeds that have been waiting for a new and warmer season to grow.

Doesn't it all make sense now? The examples given of nature's seasons give us insight into our own seasons of life.

Can you relate to ever feeling like your circumstances in life had changed to the point that they lost their usual color or vibrancy? Things and people you once held close seemed to have fallen away. Or maybe you've felt sometimes like you were frozen in time and space and lying dormant. No growth. . . no progress. Then all of sudden . . . BAM! HERE COMES A MIGHTY RUSHING WIND. Appearing to come only to make matters worse.

Be encouraged. Just like in nature, know that your winds come to remove the debris that has been covering the seeds that God has been preserving for your new season. Though your season may seem uncertain and unfamiliar, know that the rain in your storm won't drown you or kill you. It's gonna water the seed that's been waiting for it. It's gonna wake up those things that have been held back in the roots since everything fell off. What you face might appear dead, but you will see growth again. You are going to see maturity and a harvest. Don't give up!

Some of your old things must pass away in order for you to claim your NEW SEASON.

TFT: What season do you believe you're in? Would you consider it a season of winter, spring, summer, or fall?

My thoughts for today...

_____

_____

_____

_____

_____

_____

_____

_____

_____

_____

_____

_____

_____

_____

_____

_____

_____

_____

_____

_____

_____

_____

_____

_____

_____

Conclude with G.R.A.C.E.

G.R.A.C.E.

Use the acronym G.R.A.C.E to reflect on today's lesson.

G. What are you most grateful for today?

_____

_____

_____

R. As you reflect back on today's lesson, what remains on your mind and why?

_____

_____

A. What could YOU have done differently? What would need to change in order to get better results?

_____

_____

C. Commune - This is your time to pray and communicate with God. You can write it or say it aloud; but at least write down key points, so you can keep a record of your conversation and concern for God.

_____

_____

E. Based on today's lesson what action do you need to take?

_____

_____

That person is like a tree planted by streams of water, which yields its FRUIT in season and whose leaf does not wither— whatever they do PROSPERS.

~ PSALM 1:3 ~

Day Six

Keep Watching!
God Is Doing Something Great!

1 This is the message that the Lord revealed to the prophet Habakkuk.
Habakkuk Complains of Injustice
2 O Lord, how long must I call for help before you listen, before you
save us from violence? 3 Why do you make me see such trouble? How
can you stand to look on such wrongdoing? Destruction and violence
are all around me, and there is fighting and quarreling everywhere. 4
The law is weak and useless, and justice is never done. Evil people get
the better of the righteous, and so justice is perverted.
The Lord's Reply
5 Then the Lord said to his people, "Keep watching the nations around
you, and you will be astonished at what you see. I am going to do
something that you will not believe when you hear about it.
~Habakkuk 1:1-5 (GNT)~

Today, I want to draw our attention to the sovereignty of our Great God.

I'm pretty sure most of us believe God to be great. We probably refer to Him as great. We agree with others that He is great. But can I ask the question? Do you really know He's great?

Seriously?! Do you know the Lord is great? Have you reverenced Him as great? In your daily walking, your eating, your sleeping, in your everyday coming and going... Can the life you live publicly exemplify the greatness of God?

I walked outside one day just as it was beginning to rain. I could see the clouds moving just above me, and they had begun to show dark, and then shortly after the rain started.

As I began to absorb what I was witnessing, I started to reflect...

When it comes to rainy days, typically, we are more observant and prepared for physical rains than we are for spiritual ones.

You see, in terms of physical rain, we listen to the reports. We listen to how bad the rain will be this time. Then, depending on the report, we might choose whether or not we're going to go out for the day. We may choose, rather, to stay inside.

If we do choose to go outside, we'll usually take an umbrella, a raincoat or poncho, or even rain boots; so that if the rain is said to be significant our feet won't become wet when we walk out into the environment.

Quite carefully, during physical rain, we do our best to stay covered up and watch where we step. This is not always the case when it comes to spiritual rain. No no no . . . Oftentimes, we are completely unprepared for spiritual rain.

So, going back to my observation. . . As I stood outside, I thought to myself... Most of the time when we experience physical rain, though we might take precautions, we actually don't consider everything that must remain in alignment for the rain to fall.

You see. . . If we think about it from the viewpoint of science, there are certain conditions that must be in place for rain to come. There must be certain movements, temperatures, and pressure acting together to cause the change in weather. Their alignment is critical to the conditions that will manifest. But note, although the storm and rain may come, there are other components that won't change.

During the rain, the sun won't run away or lose its position. The stars won't scatter to different places because they heard the thunder. The moon won't shatter into pieces because of the lightning strikes.

Noooo. On the contrary, everything will be in its place; because it is attuned to not only God's alignment but also His divine assignment.

And so, I hope that you're able to understand that regardless of how you walk out into this everyday life, God has an alignment and an assignment specifically for you.

So when your rain returns (and it will), you have to be postured to endure. With that said, know that you must remain prepared by praying to God, staying in His Word, and staying connected to other strong believers in the faith. When the troubles of life come, you can't run or be afraid. You must remain steadfast and unmovable. Yes, of course, adjust and take precautions, but as you walk into unfamiliar spiritual environments COVER UP. How do you do that spiritually? By grabbing your spiritual raincoat, umbrella, and rain boots. Everything that is meant to keep you safe.

What protection do you need?

Ephesians 6:10 calls it the WHOLE ARMOR OF GOD:
- Helmet of Salvation
- Breastplate of Righteousness
- Belt of Truth
- Shoes shod with the Gospel of Peace
- Shield of Faith
- Sword of the Spirit
- Prayer and Supplication

The scripture tells us in verses 10-12 that we are to uniform ourselves in this attire daily so that we may be able to withstand in the evil day..."

In other words, we should prepare ourselves to expect rain and bad weather every day. We should never be caught unprepared. But be assured, even in the midst of strange clouds gathering in your life, there are great things that have been aligned and assigned just for you.

Just KEEP WATCHING. You will be astonished at what you see. God is going to do something that you will not believe when you hear about it. And the best part is . . .He's doing it for you.

_____

TFT: What new thing can you sense that God is doing for you?

My thoughts for today...

G.R.A.C.E.

Use the acronym G.R.A.C.E to reflect on today's lesson.

G. What are you most grateful for today?

_____

_____

_____

R. As you reflect back on today's lesson, what remains on your mind and why?

_____

_____

A. What could YOU have done differently? What would need to change in order to get better results?

_____

_____

C. Commune - This is your time to pray and communicate with God. You can write it or say it aloud; but at least write down key points, so you can keep a record of your conversation and concern for God.

_____

_____

E. Based on today's lesson what action do you need to take?

_____

_____

Behold
all things
have become
NEW
2 CORINTHIANS 5:17

NEW DAY OF G.R.A.C.E.

Day Seven

Go Ahead. Ask!

Therefore I tell you, whatever you ask for in prayer,
believe that you have received it, and it will be yours.
~Mark 11:24 (NKJV)~
(Minister Ashley Thomas - Contributing Author)

For some, asking for anything (particularly help) from anyone is a hard task. Some find it so difficult that even when it comes to asking God to provide for their needs and desires it is a struggle; even though they may still profess Him to be sovereign (possessing supreme or ultimate power above and over all things). Some people are hesitant to ask God for anything because they feel unworthy or fear that their imperfections may result in unanswered prayers.

One might ask themselves some of these questions:

- How do I know what I'm asking for is in His will?
- How do I know what I'm asking for isn't too much?
- How do I know it will be done?"

Have confidence that our sovereign God is able and willing to answer your prayers. When our heart changes and we are drawn toward God, our desires change. As we die to our flesh and become more alive in the spirit, the posture of our heart changes; therefore what we ask for in Jesus' name changes too.

43

The Holy Spirit within us knows what God is thinking. First Corinthians 2:11 tells us "For what person knows the thoughts and motives of a man except the man's spirit within him? So also no one knows the thoughts of God except the Spirit of God."

As the Holy Spirit guides us and ministers to us, it aids us in our thoughts. The more in tune we are with the spirit, we realize that our once negative, doubtful, self-defeating, or even unloving thoughts begin to align with God's character and the Fruit of the Spirit – love, joy, peace, patience, kindness, goodness, faithfulness, gentleness, and self-control– (Galatians 5:22). With that said, our desires and our requests begin to align to God's will for our lives.

So, my friend, don't let the devil talk you out of asking for anything that your heart desires! God is able and willing and He loves knowing that we trust and believe Him to be who He says He is. Therefore, if you know your heart is postured toward the Lord, you are free to ask of ANYTHING in Jesus' name. Amen!
~Minister Ashley Thomas

TFT: What are you afraid to ask of God? Why?

My thoughts for today...

_____

_____

_____

_____

_____

_____

_____

_____

_____

_____

_____

_____

_____

_____

_____

_____

_____

_____

_____

_____

_____

_____

_____

Conclude with G.R.A.C.E.

G.R.A.C.E.

Use the acronym G.R.A.C.E to reflect on today's lesson.

G. What are you most grateful for today?

_____

_____

_____

R. As you reflect back on today's lesson, what remains on your mind and why?

_____

_____

A. What could YOU have done differently? What would need to change in order to get better results?

_____

_____

C. Commune - This is your time to pray and communicate with God. You can write it or say it aloud; but at least write down key points, so you can keep a record of your conversation and concern for God.

_____

_____

E. Based on today's lesson what action do you need to take?

_____

_____

The Lord said, "I will go with you, and I will give you victory."

~Exodus 33:14~

Day Eight

Just Say the Word

And Mary said,
Behold the handmaid of the Lord;
be it unto me according to thy word.
And the angel departed from her.
~Luke 1:38 (KJV)~

I know I've probably said this for every scripture so far, but this, too, is one of my all time favorites. Mary, after being informed by the angel that she has been chosen by God to give birth to the Messiah, responded,

". . . be it unto me according to thy word."

This phrase is on I repeat to myself anytime I feel the Holy Spirit's guiding that God is calling me to something that is foreign to my wheelhouse – those things that I have already mastered or am at least familiar with. No, I repeat this when God is introducing me to something I haven't yet considered, or an idea that I hadn't already planned out in some fashion. Maybe it has subconsciously been a desire, but not yet an actionable plan. When I feel that little twinge inside of me that says, "Dawn, this is for you. Go ahead. God's got you." Yeah. . . that little voice within, pushing me outside of my comfort zone. When that happens, I whisper to myself, "Be it unto me according to thy word."

First off, can we go back and just try to process what was being presented to Mary – a teenage girl betrothed to her

48

fiance, Joseph, whom she had never known. Meaning . . . They had never had sex. Yes, this young girl, who had never been with a man intimately, is being told (by an angel, no less) that the Holy Spirit is going to come upon her and impregnate her with a living child. This is definitely pre-mental health era; because Mary would have surely been a candidate for self-referral. What she is being presented with is unimaginable. Only a crazy woman would believe it. Or . . . You'd have to have some crazy faith.

Let's understand, when you're "chosen" by God, like Mary was, to birth something new that the world has not yet heard of, man does not have to "touch it" for it to come forth. Neither does man need to validate whether you're the right selection. Trust me, it's coming forth because God is in it.
I know that there are people who we hope would be with us, to come alongside us on our journey to newness; but there is a limit to how many people can be in the birthing room.

Let me tell you what I was told when my husband and I were starting ministry. We knew without a shadow of a doubt that God had called us, but we were a little disappointed that certain people weren't there to support us as we expected. Then one night after a Bible study, a visiting church mother grabbed me and hugged me, and said, "Daughter, when God is birthing something new in you, everybody can't be your midwife."

Her words sent chills through me.

I pulled away and looked in her face with an expression like, "How did you know?"

In turn, she continued in saying, "And once God has birthed through you what He's called you to do, everybody can't babysit."

Talk about revelation!

From that moment forward, I released those people I was holding hostage to my thoughts and opinions, and I stopped being concerned with who was supporting me and my husband. As long as God was leading us and we were listening, He would connect us and put us exactly where we were to be.

". . .be it unto me according to thy word."

I hope my encounter encourages you too. Be confident that if God has given you the vision, or called you into something that seems strange, unimaginable, and impossible for others to put their minds around, go with God and not what anyone else is saying. God doesn't need certain people, properties, or logistics to be in place to bring forth what He's birthing through us. Keep in mind, all of creation was manifested from NOTHING because He spoke a word to "let there be . . ." Mary said, ". . . be it unto me according to thy word." Though the angel brought Mary the word, as the Church Mother did with me, the message was from the Lord.

What word has God brought to you about what He wants to birth from you that you're sitting on?

Finally, consider this while you're carrying the gift of what God impregnated you with, to birth in due season . . . It will come forth in DUE SEASON. Beloved, when are you due?

The scripture implies to us that Mary went through a full-term pregnancy. We don't get anywhere that she had complications (other than running for her life) or had Jesus prematurely. No. Jesus came right on schedule. Take that as an indicator. Whatever God has given you to carry in this season to birth . . know that it has an appointed time. Be careful with it. Don't abort it; don't miscarry it, and don't try to birth it prematurely. Let it mature within you so that it can bring forth the life that God intended. Consider this your official Baby Shower. "Be it unto YOU according to HIS word!"

TFT: What is God birthing in you in this New Season?

Thought For Today!

My thoughts for today...

_____

_____

_____

_____

_____

_____

_____

_____

_____

_____

_____

_____

_____

_____

_____

_____

_____

_____

_____

_____

_____

_____

_____

_____

Conclude with G.R.A.C.E.

G.R.A.C.E.

Use the acronym G.R.A.C.E to reflect on today's lesson.

G. What are you most grateful for today?

_____

_____

_____

R. As you reflect back on today's lesson, what remains on your mind and why?

_____

_____

A. What could YOU have done differently? What would need to change in order to get better results?

_____

_____

C. Commune - This is your time to pray and communicate with God. You can write it or say it aloud; but at least write down key points, so you can keep a record of your conversation and concern for God.

_____

_____

E. Based on today's lesson what action do you need to take?

_____

_____

"MY *Grace* is sufficient for YOU, for my power is made PERFECT in weakness."

~ 2 Corinthians 12:9~

Day Nine

God's Strength Will Be Your Portion

My flesh and my heart faileth:
but God is the strength of my heart,
and my portion forever.
~Psalm 73:26 (KJV)~

Today is a revisit of the scripture presented on Day Two but from a different perspective. I love that lessons can be illumined from the same scripture to give us encouragement and guidance as we mature in our mindset. As we grow and experience life, scriptures that we've read or heard over and over will begin to have new meanings. With that said, let's focus on the ending of Psalm 73:26.

Have you ever just been tired? No, I mean really tired.? Like, not just tired in your physical body, but even tired in your mind and thoughts . . . in your entire being. Every aspect of what you do and who you are is consuming you from every angle.

Simply put, life is just happening, and you're tired.

Sometimes you don't even know how you will go on. IF. . .you will go on. There are days you just want to throw in the towel and say, "You win!" to whoever "You" is –spouse, children, parents, boss, co-workers, church. . .

In today's passage of scripture, David was tired and frustrated with people, and even God. What?! You didn't think we could also be frustrated with God?

Look, the Bible tells us that David was a man after God's own heart. God loved and esteemed David. So, if David could even have moments of frustration with life and the God he loved, how much more do you think that we might?

Let me tell you, I have had my share of life battles and being tired. To name a few, I began having convulsive seizures at the age of five. I was in an abusive relationship as a teen and struggled with self-esteem. I was misunderstood in college. Became a single mother in my twenties. Had very public difficulties in my marriage in my 30s. Went through three miscarriages between 40-45. Had "daddy issues" from birth until I was 48 years old. Then, I had to give up a career I absolutely loved to focus on the behavioral and cognitive challenges of my adoptive child.

Oh yeah! I've been tired.

Yet, through everything I faced. . .and though at times I questioned God's intention for my life. . . some kinda strange way. . . I trusted His plan for me. Mainly because, despite all my challenges, I still knew and believed God to be faithful. That last paragraph was a snapshot of some of the challenges I faced. I promise you, the prayers answered and the ways God has made for me and my family can't be summed up into a paragraph quite as singularly. But I'll at least give you a synopsis of what I mentioned.

God healed me of seizures when I was 10 years old. Haven't had one since. I am married to a wonderfully amazing husband who loves and fears the Lord; who adores his family and who provides significantly and unselfishly for them. The son (born to that once single mother) is an amazingly talented, athletic, musically inclined, college graduate; who attended college on both full academic and athletic scholarships.

God has allowed me to minister to and provide resources to a number of women who have lost pregnancies, or who had difficulties becoming pregnant, and give them hope to trust God despite their disappointments. My biological dad and I reconciled all unresolved issues, and God afforded me the opportunity to be at his side until his dying day. And finally, for the career I would have never left, God repositioned me back into my first love of writing and allowed me to publish not only devotions to encourage other women...but also a successful children's book that addresses the very issue that was at the helm of why I had to leave my other job in the first place.

Oh yeah! Despite all my difficulties and frustrations, past and present, I continue to trust God.

Yes, through my life experiences, "my flesh and my heart [at times have] faileth, but God [was and] is the strength of my heart, and my portion forever.

Before I conclude, I do still want to bring attention to the last "portion" of the scripture. The word "portion." Portion by definition has to do with parts of a whole that have already been divided. Portion can also relate to one receiving an inheritance. Honestly, both meanings give me encouragement.

If we consider that the inheritance God has for us has already been divided into portions that we can manageably consume, and that he is with us and strengthening us along the way, we might better understand why our progress through life has to take an intentional path and pace.

The portions that have been created for you now will lead to the WHOLE version of you. What you are experiencing now are merely fragments of something, or rather someone, greater.

So, here is to embracing your WHOLENESS journey. Enjoy each portion as it comes.

TFT: How do you feel knowing God has a portion established for you?

My thoughts for today...

_____

_____

_____

_____

_____

_____

_____

_____

_____

_____

_____

_____

_____

_____

_____

_____

_____

_____

_____

_____

_____

_____

_____

_____

Conclude with G.R.A.C.E.

G.R.A.C.E.

Use the acronym G.R.A.C.E to reflect on today's lesson.

G. What are you most grateful for today?

_____

_____

_____

R. As you reflect back on today's lesson, what remains on your mind and why?

_____

_____

A. What could YOU have done differently? What would need to change in order to get better results?

_____

_____

C. Commune - This is your time to pray and communicate with God. You can write it or say it aloud; but at least write down key points, so you can keep a record of your conversation and concern for God.

_____

_____

E. Based on today's lesson what action do you need to take?

_____

_____

Some **TRUST** in chariots, and some in horses: **but we will** remember the name of the Lord our **GOD.**

~Psalm 20:7~

NEW DAY OF G.R.A.C.E.

Day Ten

You Can Trust God

Trust in the Lord with all thine heart;
and lean not unto thine own understanding.
In all thy ways acknowledge him,
and he shall direct thy paths.
~Proverbs 3:5-6 (KJV)~

I know that when we're in the midst of a struggle, it can be hard to trust God. Our first instinct is to try to figure it out or fix it. Or, to retreat and hide away from the reality of what the situation has created. But be assured that even in the midst of adversity you can trust God.

Jeremiah 29:11 tells us that He alone knows the plan that He has for our lives. Plans to prosper us and give us a hope and a future, and not disaster. So know that regardless of what you may face, this place was not meant to destroy you but to grow you so that you will be better equipped with strength and wisdom in your next season.

I know we might feel like our life experiences have given us the supreme expertise to assess our situation and handle it on our own, and in our own power; but I'm again reminded of the scripture that says, "Not by might. Not by power, but by the spirit of the Lord." (Zechariah 4:6)

Listen, we alone don't have enough strength or wisdom to outthink God, nor His plan or purpose for us concerning any matter. Only God knows; therefore, we must trust Him.

If we acknowledge Him in everything we do, He will direct us in the way that we should go. Matthew 6:33 tells us to seek first the Kingdom of God and His righteousness and all these things shall be added unto us.

What are all these things you ask? We might initially think that they are all the material things that our heart desires; but honestly, once we're aligned with God and in daily communion with Him, His will becomes the desire that we not only seek but can be satisfied with.

If trusting someone outside yourself is something that you are not accustomed to because you've been hurt or feel unappreciated, or have been taken advantage of by others in the past, or maybe you just have trust or control issues. . . can I make a suggestion? Trust God. You won't be disappointed.

———————————

TFT: Do you trust God and His plan for you even if it's not clear at this time?

My thoughts for today...

_____

_____

_____

_____

_____

_____

_____

_____

_____

_____

_____

_____

_____

_____

_____

_____

_____

_____

_____

_____

_____

_____

_____

Conclude with G.R.A.C.E.

G.R.A.C.E.

Use the acronym G.R.A.C.E to reflect on today's lesson.

G. What are you most grateful for today?

_____

_____

_____

R. As you reflect back on today's lesson, what remains on your mind and why?

_____

_____

A. What could YOU have done differently? What would need to change in order to get better results?

_____

_____

C. Commune - This is your time to pray and communicate with God. You can write it or say it aloud; but at least write down key points, so you can keep a record of your conversation and concern for God.

_____

_____

E. Based on today's lesson what action do you need to take?

_____

_____

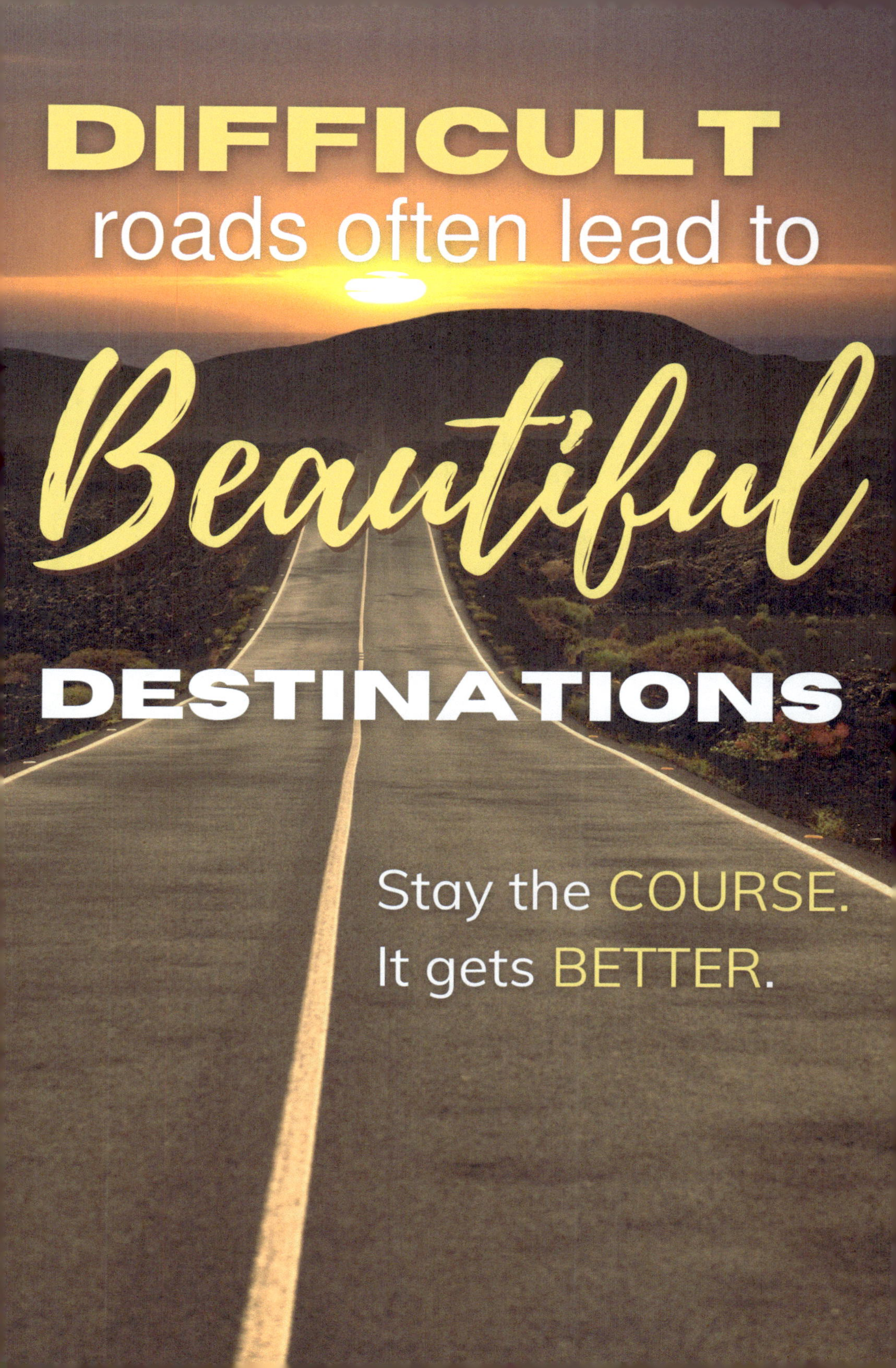
DIFFICULT
roads often lead to
Beautiful
DESTINATIONS
Stay the COURSE.
It gets BETTER.

Day Eleven

Learn the Rotation

The Lord is my shepherd; I shall not want.
He maketh me to lie down in green pastures:
he leadeth me beside the still waters.
He restoreth my soul:
he leadeth me in the paths of righteousness
for his name's sake.
Yea, though I walk through the valley of the shadow of death,
I will fear no evil: for thou art with me;
thy rod and thy staff they comfort me.
Thou preparest a table before me
in the presence of mine enemies:
thou anointest my head with oil;
my cup runneth over.
Surely goodness and mercy shall follow me all the days of my life:
and I will dwell in the house of the Lord forever.
~Psalm 23 (KJV)~

I often share my belief that we all are in a constant rotation of the 23rd Psalm. Think about it. We are either in the green pastures experiencing the abundance, beside the still waters resting and getting restoration or on assignment towards the path of our purpose.

But as scripture tells us, after we get on the path toward our purpose, the next stop is the "valley of the shadow of death." But as my husband made clear in a message, it's the valley of the 'shadow' of death. It doesn't say 'the valley of death,' but rather, the shadow of it. You got that, right? It's a shadow, y'all! Don't be afraid. It just appears bigger than it is.

But I'll take it a step further now and add... How do you get SHADOWS in a valley? Well, it's simple. In order for the valley to cast a shadow, there must be lights.

Be assured, my friend. God brought you to this place, and His light guides you just in the direction you're supposed to be going. Don't be afraid. The valley isn't intended to destroy you. It's intended to teach you and build your faith and confidence.

"...thy rod and thy staff, they comfort me." ~ Psalm 23:4
You see! We learn lessons in the valley. And no matter how we might try, it's impossible to avoid the valley experiences. Do you know why? The valley is the only way to get to the table.

You might ask, "What's so significant about getting to the table?" Well, the table is where we get our heads anointed. The anointing, you see, brings renewed strength as well as new assignments. You don't think God would put you through testing for nothing, do you? Always know that God doesn't waste our time; but, rather, He prepares us.

Whatever hardships you face in your valley are strengthening you for what is ahead. Have confidence in knowing goodness and mercy follow us to our next assignment once we leave the table. Fortunately, the Good Shepherd is providing us with direction, and we go back through the process all over again – abundance, restoration, journey, valley, table, anointing, and new assignment. REPEAT.

The assignment God has for you in your next season requires more maturity and growth, so don't despise the process. Embrace it...each and every time.

———————————

TFT: Where are you in your 23rd Psalm experience?

My thoughts for today...

_____
_____
_____
_____
_____
_____
_____
_____
_____
_____
_____
_____
_____
_____
_____
_____
_____
_____
_____
_____
_____
_____
_____
_____
_____
_____

Conclude with G.R.A.C.E.

G.R.A.C.E.

Use the acronym G.R.A.C.E to reflect on today's lesson.

G. What are you most grateful for today?

_____

_____

_____

R. As you reflect back on today's lesson, what remains on your mind and why?

_____

_____

A. What could YOU have done differently? What would need to change in order to get better results?

_____

_____

C. Commune - This is your time to pray and communicate with God. You can write it or say it aloud; but at least write down key points, so you can keep a record of your conversation and concern for God.

_____

_____

E. Based on today's lesson what action do you need to take?

_____

_____

"

REMEMBER,
AS YOU WALK THROUGH
THE VALLEY...
IT HAS A SHADOW.
THAT MEANS...
IT HAS LIGHTS.
STAY THE COURSE.

dawn

"

Day Twelve

Never Forsaken

I have been young, and now am old;
yet have I not seen the righteous forsaken,
nor his seed begging bread.
~Psalm 37:25 (KJV)~
(Pastor Leon J. Green, Jr. - Contributing Author)

As a child growing up in New Orleans, I had the privilege of living next door to my grandparents. Grandma, Mary Lee Potter, was my favorite. Grandma worked as a pastry baker at the A&P Warehouse. She had a very loving and kind nature, not just toward the family, but to almost everyone she encountered.

I never saw Grandma leave for work in the mornings, but I would often see her walking home carrying armloads of bread. Mind you, the walk was about three miles away, which might not seem like a long way in everyday perspective, but for a woman of seasoned age, I thought it was too far.

One day while sitting at her kitchen table, I remember asking, "Grandma, why don't you catch the bus carrying all that bread?"

Now let's just be clear, Mary-Lee Potter was no-nonsense regarding God, her family, and her birds (she was a bird enthusiast of her time).

To my question, Grandma insisted that, though the walk seemed a bit long, and carrying her loaves could have been made easier by riding the bus; she insisted that walking was her ministry and her special time with God. Besides, she said she would much rather walk the distance talking with God than be vexed or demeaned by being subjected to riding the back of the bus.

One of Grandma's favorite scriptures was Psalm 37:25.

As an old man, King David testified that he had never seen the righteous abandoned, nor had ever witnessed their children hungry for bread.

My grandmother was a woman of great faith, and that was always evident in how she treated others. She always gave of herself to her children and usually had something special tucked away for her grandchildren. And even though Grandma wasn't a rich woman by any means, it seemed she somehow had more than enough for herself, us, her birds, and anyone else whom she knew was in need; plus, an overflow. Do you want to know how? Of course, most of it had to do with those conversations with God, but also... those armloads of bread. Those loaves of bread helped feed her family, her friends and neighbors, strangers, and as I'm sure you guessed...the birds.

While my grandmother was walking back and forth to work with her loaves of bread, her intimate conversations with the Lord were ordering her steps safely along her life's path in a way that delighted him. Psalm 37:4, tells us, "Delight yourself in the Lord, and he will give you the desires of your heart." Grandma's desire to show her love and to help others was fulfilled because of how she made time for God. Even though she could have easily ridden the bus, she didn't want to put herself in a position that would have caused her to dishonor God or others; whether out loud or in her spirit. So, she chose to walk with the Lord both literally and figuratively.

As you continue your journey to reclaiming your newness every day, be encouraged to follow God, and be compelled to bless others who are less fortunate than you. And know this, regardless of your situation (good or bad, lack or plenty) there are always others less fortunate than you. Take the lead from Grandma. When you walk with God and share your bread with others (whatever your bread might be); know that not only will you receive blessings back to you, but your children and grandchildren to the next generations will benefit.

Here's to making your NEW DAY someone else's as well. ~Pastor, Leon J. Green, Jr.

TFT: How do you, or how could you, share your gifts, talents, or time with others?

My thoughts for today...

G.R.A.C.E.

Use the acronym G.R.A.C.E to reflect on today's lesson.

G. What are you most grateful for today?

_____

_____

_____

R. As you reflect back on today's lesson, what remains on your mind and why?

_____

_____

A. What could YOU have done differently? What would need to change in order to get better results?

_____

_____

C. Commune - This is your time to pray and communicate with God. You can write it or say it aloud; but at least write down key points, so you can keep a record of your conversation and concern for God.

_____

_____

E. Based on today's lesson what action do you need to take?

_____

_____

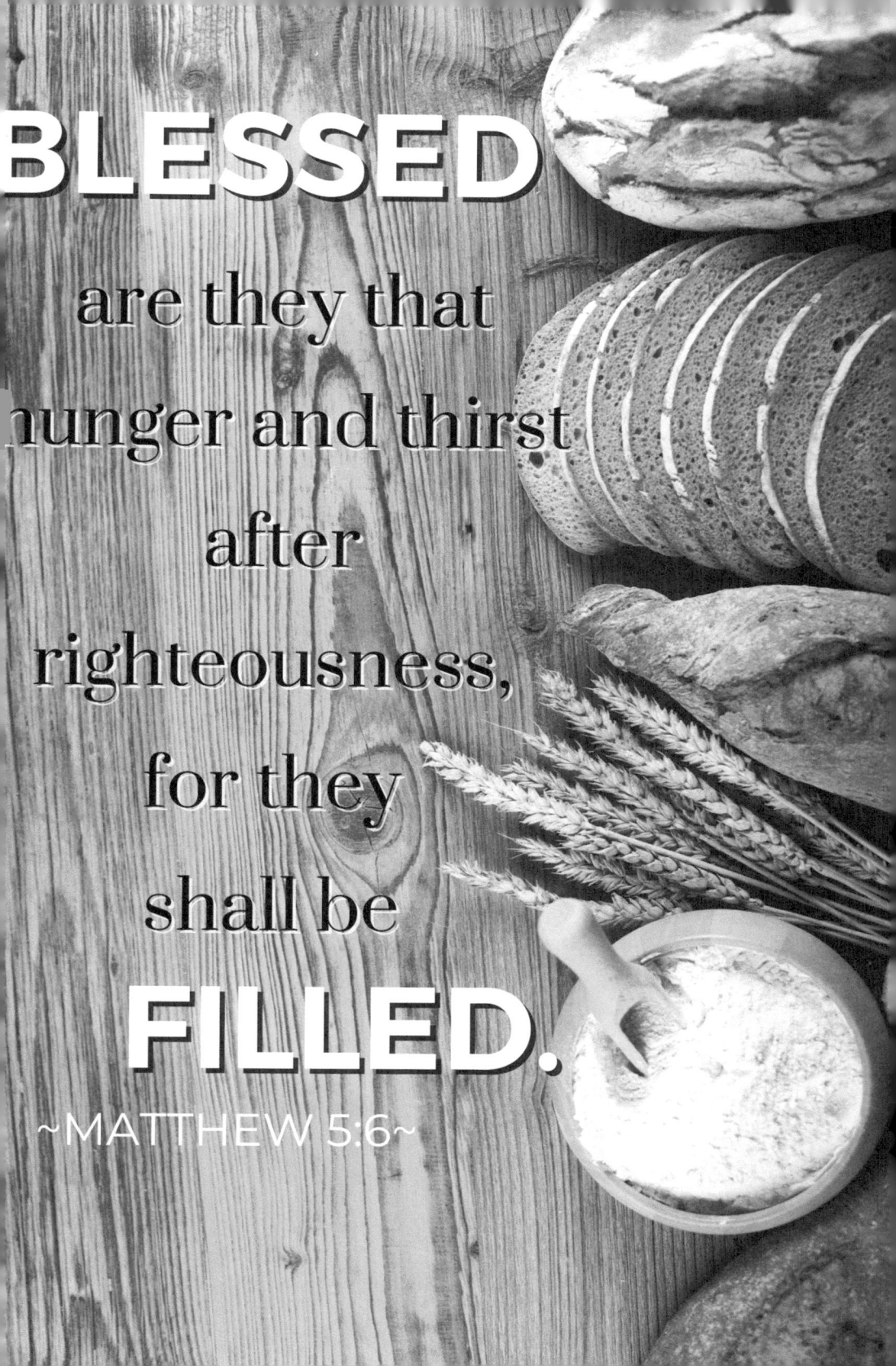

BLESSED are they that hunger and thirst after righteousness, for they shall be **FILLED.**

~MATTHEW 5:6~

Day Thirteen

What Remains is ENOUGH

And they did all eat, and were filled:
and they took up of the fragments that remained
twelve baskets full.
~Matthew 14:20 (KJV)~

Matthew 14 is probably a familiar scripture to you, whether you're a Bible scholar or not. This chapter of scripture is the account of Jesus feeding the 5,000 with only two fish and five loaves of bread. That imagery in itself is enough to get you excited about the possibilities of what God is able to do.

In my opinion, this not only speaks to Him being able to do something new; but also His ability to be able to make something enormous from mere crumbs. So, it should be an example to all of us that God is able to provide for our needs, no matter what they may be.

However, what I found most fascinating about this passage was not what was done for the 5,000, but rather what was done and shown to the twelve disciples.

The disciples thought it would have been a better idea for Jesus to send the people away so that the 13 of them could rest and get something to eat. It had been a long day and they were tired of serving all these needy people. Plus, it would have been logistically impossible for them to feed all these men, women, and children.

Can you relate to how the disciples were feeling? Tired of serving. Tired of being there for other people. Tired of always being available when no one seems to ever be available to you in the same way? Fear that if you continue to give to everyone else you will somehow miss out on having what you so desperately want and need?

But, rather than take the disciples' advice to dismiss the people, Jesus told them to gather the people together and feed them.

I can only imagine they were probably like, "Jesus, you do realize that we are hungry too and have nothing. AND... there are 5,000 of these people following us. We're tired; and how are we supposed to feed them? With what?!"

Well, the passage tells us that Jesus took the two fish and five loaves that they got from a little boy; He blessed it, broke it, and miraculously actually fed all the people.

That seems to be indicative of how God deals with us too. Just when we're at our wit's end, He tells us to stand fast, give Him what we have (even though it seems like it's nothing), and trust Him to perform a miracle. We feel as though if we continue to give of ourselves there will be nothing left for us...or of us. But the conclusion of the passage gives a different example.

After the disciples served the 5,000, they were to go around and pick up the remnants. Coincidentally, there were 12 full baskets left. How many baskets? How many disciples? You get my point.

When you're with Jesus (communing with Him through prayer and scripture) and trusting Him with your minimum, along with your tiredness and frustrations, He will always make sure that you have just what you need.

So this encounter was not just an act for the people to take away to understand how great Jesus was; it was also an act to REMIND the twelve of His great power as well.

Please find encouragement here too. God knows your tiredness. He knows how much you've committed yourself to other people, and how sometimes you feel you'll miss the things you need because of it. Know that there is more than enough and that God always has you in mind.

_____

TFT: What are you afraid that you don't have enough of but that God keeps continuing to provide for you?

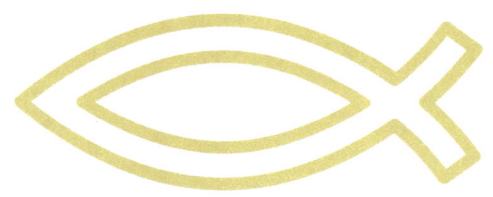

My thoughts for today...

_____

_____

_____

_____

_____

_____

_____

_____

_____

_____

_____

_____

_____

_____

_____

_____

_____

_____

_____

_____

_____

_____

_____

_____

Conclude with G.R.A.C.E.

G.R.A.C.E.

Use the acronym G.R.A.C.E to reflect on today's lesson.

G. What are you most grateful for today?

_____

_____

R. As you reflect back on today's lesson, what remains on your mind and why?

_____

_____

A. What could YOU have done differently? What would need to change in order to get better results?

_____

_____

C. Commune - This is your time to pray and communicate with God. You can write it or say it aloud; but at least write down key points, so you can keep a record of your conversation and concern for God.

_____

_____

E. Based on today's lesson what action do you need to take?

_____

_____

Day Fourteen

God's Word is Sufficient for You

So shall my word be that goeth forth out of my mouth:
it shall not return unto me void,
but it shall accomplish that which I please,
and it shall prosper in the thing whereto I sent it
~Isaiah 55:11 (KJV)~

Have you ever had to void a check? If you have, it was either for one of a few reasons. One reason could have been, you needed to share your account information to set up a payment, but you wanted to avoid anyone being able to write against the check an amount you didn't authorize. So, you would write or stamp the check as VOID. Another reason could be, the check had already been used electronically, but you needed to avoid mistakenly using the check number again, which might cause the bank to flag your account, and not honor the check. This could also create an issue with whomever you intended to pay.

Additionally, maybe you needed to void a check in the unfortunate occurrence that you either made the check out to the wrong person or wrote the check for the wrong amount. Consequently, you would either need to void the check immediately and write a corrected one. Or, if the check had already gone out, you would need to contact your financial institution to have them stop payment on the check and not honor it once it was received to be cashed.

If something is void, it is defined as having no legal value; being without specification; useless; or empty. In the scripture passage, God is speaking through Isaiah the Prophet to the people of Israel that whatever He speaks will not return void – having no value, without specification, useless, or empty. He assures that not only will it have value, be specific, have use, and substance; but, it cannot fail, and will also accomplish whatever He said it would.

That's a big promise!

But our BIG FATHER can have the confidence to make this kind of promise to His children. And I love the analogy He associates with it to prove His point in verse 10 when He says,

"My word is like the snow and the rain
that come down from the sky to water the earth.
They make the crops grow
and provide seed for planting and food to eat.
~Isaiah 55:10 (GNT)~

Then He goes straight into..."SO ALSO will be the word that I speak. It WILL NOT return void." God's word will do what He planned for it, and accomplish what it was sent to do. That's not only deep...but powerful. God is letting it be known upfront that EVERYTHING He sends has a purpose; and if we ask anything in His name, restating the words He has already promised...those words cannot return back to Him and He deny them. Numbers 23:19 (GNT) tells us, "God is not like people, who lie; He is not a human who changes his mind. Whatever he promises, he does; He speaks, and it is done."

I don't know what else I can say on this matter. The scripture literally speaks for itself. It is truly alive and active.

You'll never have to worry, God's words will never bounce or have insufficient funds. You'll never need to worry whether you'll need to contact someone else because you feel you misspoke and need someone to stop your words from getting to Heaven. God wants to do great things for you, and He wants you to expect it and call Him out on it.

So what are you waiting for? Ask whatever you want according to His word and believe that the best will come.

TFT: What steps do you take to make sure your word is not void?

My thoughts for today...

G.R.A.C.E.

Use the acronym G.R.A.C.E to reflect on today's lesson.

G. What are you most grateful for today?

_____

_____

_____

R. As you reflect back on today's lesson, what remains on your mind and why?

_____

_____

A. What could YOU have done differently? What would need to change in order to get better results?

_____

_____

C. Commune - This is your time to pray and communicate with God. You can write it or say it aloud; but at least write down key points, so you can keep a record of your conversation and concern for God.

_____

_____

E. Based on today's lesson what action do you need to take?

_____

_____

"For as the rain comes down, and the snow from heaven, And do not return there, But water the earth, And make it bring forth and bud, That it may give seed to the sower And bread to the eater,

So shall My word be that goes forth from My mouth; It shall not return to Me void, But it shall accomplish what I please, And it shall prosper in the thing for which I sent it." ~Isaiah 55:10-11~

Day Fifteen

Strength & Conditioning

But they that wait upon the Lord shall renew their strength;
they shall mount up with wings as eagles;
they shall run, and not be weary;
and they shall walk, and not faint.
~Isaiah 40:31 (KJV)~
(Rudy A. Valentine, III - Contributing Author)

What is the definition of revival? Revival is the improvement of the strength and condition of something.

As a college athlete, preparing for competition was paramount. However, the goal was never to just perform. The goal was to work to become an elite force. This approach to preparation is not just true for athletes but for anyone serious about the role that they operate in or aspire to become. One can aspire to be great in their career, as a spouse or parent, a student, or as a Christian. The goal is to work to be the greatest version of what you can be, but understand that in order to be great. . . just like an athlete. . . you're going to need some strength and conditioning.

Strength and conditioning are pivotal to the process of the greatest-known athletes. Yes! Those names we know best like Michael Jordan and Lebron James (and so many others) seem to have always been naturally talented and possessed the skill to perform well; but without regular strength and conditioning, neither of them could have risen to the heights which they did for so long and continued to have competed with other athletes half their age.

If you look at any great athletic program, so much credit and attention are placed on the regular season, as well as the athletes and coaches. But, if we really were able to look behind the success holistically, attention would have to be given to strength and conditioning training done before and after practice, or in the off-season. Honestly, that's where most of the discipline and work is happening that creates the dynamic athletes we have come to know and recognize.

We should consider this approach even as Christians. If we are hoping to revive - improve our strength and condition - in areas of our lives, we must be willing to put in the necessary work; even during those times when we can't see the evidence of what God is doing. The reality is, God is our strength and conditioning coach. He is strategically putting us through what seems like difficulties, tests, and hardships to improve our strength and conditioning. We mistake these trials often as the work of the enemy, but my thought is that we often give the enemy too much credit. For sometimes, the struggles placed on us are strategically orchestrated by God.

So often we want blessings; we want to reach certain goals; we have lofty desires, but, if what we wish for is more than we have the capacity to handle, we must grow through (or into) that blessing. So God will put something difficult in front of us to strengthen us, but on the other side of it is the blessing we've hoped to receive.

The improvement of our strength and conditioning is going to better us for the race we've been purposed to run.

Listen, no runner can compete well in a race without proper training. If one tries, they'll either run out of breath or experience injury.

1 Corinthians 10:13 says,

> *"Every test that you have is the kind that normally comes to people.*
> *But God keeps his promise and He will not allow you to be tested*
> *beyond your power to remain firm. (He won't put more on you than*
> *you can bear.) At the time you are put to the test, He will give you*
> *the strength to endure it and so provide you with the way out."*

The only way you're going to get out of what you face is by having the strength to endure it. Naturally, we'll want to run away from it, but we have to go through this very thing if we're going to get stronger.

Let me explain it another way. If you go to the gym and you're lifting weights and put more plates on the bar than what you're equipped to handle, without a spotter, you're going to either fall or get crushed. This example shows us that we must get stronger. We must improve our strength and conditioning so that we can handle the weight.

For us, our blessings might be the weight. A lot of times we want blessings and things that we are literally not strong enough to handle. We might want to make X amount of dollars per year, but God knows that we might not be strong enough . . . disciplined enough to handle that large of a blessing at this time. Instead, He will continue to put things in front of us meant to strengthen us so that when He does bestow our heavy blessing, we'll be strong enough to lift it.

Remember, He won't put more on you than you can bear. Just trust Him and continue to get stronger. God will condition you through and for everything you face.
~Rudolph A Valentine, III

TFT: What preparations are you making in order to carry the purpose God has in you?

My thoughts for today...

G.R.A.C.E.

Use the acronym G.R.A.C.E to reflect on today's lesson.

G. What are you most grateful for today?

_____

_____

_____

R. As you reflect back on today's lesson, what remains on your mind and why?

_____

_____

A. What could YOU have done differently? What would need to change in order to get better results?

_____

_____

C. Commune - This is your time to pray and communicate with God. You can write it or say it aloud; but at least write down key points, so you can keep a record of your conversation and concern for God.

_____

_____

E. Based on today's lesson what action do you need to take?

_____

_____

THE JOY OF THE **LORD** IS MY STRENGTH

~Nehemiah 8:10~

Day Sixteen

You've Been Forgiven

"As far as the east is from the west,
so far has He removed our transgressions from us."
~Psalm 103:12 (KJV)~
(Pastor *Anna Morris Jackson - Contributing Author*)

I enjoyed watching the movie, Woman King which starred Viola Davis. Just a side note, I predict it will receive nominations and awards for a story well told. However, at times I cringed because of the violence of the battles they fought. Not to spoil it for anyone who hasn't seen it yet, but the movie depicted a small, vibrant country in Africa whose strength lived in the power of an all-female army.

Woven throughout the movie were themes that still affect so many of our lives as women, both directly and indirectly; examples that have burdened the female throughout history. Surviving some of these difficulties requires strength, courage, and resiliency.

Personally, there were parts of the storylines that impacted me so. . . they caused my soul to look back and wonder, how I made it over.

In the movie, Viola Davis' character was one of the greatest advisors to the King. She possessed the power to see beyond the ordinary, coupled with the boldness to speak her mind, and the strength to fight for what she believed in. She and the other women of the tribe had vowed devotion to serving the king and fought willingly and determinately for the independence of their country.

At one point in her life, she had been kidnapped and sexually abused by men. As a result of that encounter, she actually became pregnant by one of her attackers. Determined to let nothing stop her from becoming a great warrior, she'd made the decision to give her baby away. This decision would be one that would continue to haunt her. And, almost 20 years later, she would learn that one of the newest, most skilled, and most determined young warriors to join their tribe was actually the child she had given away.

Throughout the movie I gained insight, shed tears, and grieved for all the women who, because of customs and opinions, were not allowed to make the best decisions for themselves and their bodies. Moreover, I walked away reflecting on my own life and some of the hard decisions I had to make as a woman; especially early on. Decisions, like the character of Viola Davis, cause women to be tormented and plagued with self-guilt.

Today, I write this devotion to anyone who may silently suffer because of little girls and boys that were not born, or if born had to be raised by someone else or given away.

Yes, I (the 70+-year-old pastor) wrote this to give voice to the eighteen-year-old me who became pregnant at the age of eighteen. And though I was the valedictorian of my high school class and was given the choice to keep my daughter, for years I still battled with the shame of becoming a teenage mother and not immediately fulfilling the dreams that I and my family had hoped for.

I am eternally grateful for the pro-choice decision I was able to make to have and keep my baby girl. I have no greater joy than that of being a mother. I thank God that I was allowed to make that decision. Yet, my heart suffers for girls and women who were not granted the opportunity to make their own decisions. To those women I say, I am truly sorry. Some may never understand how long the effects of these emotional scars will linger. My prayer is that time has or will heal you, and I sincerely offer these words of forgiveness to you with today's scripture from Psalm 103:12,

"As far as the east is from the west,
so far has He removed our transgressions from us."

As is stated in my church communion service following our prayer of confession. "In the name of Jesus Christ, you are forgiven." YOU ARE FORGIVEN.

If you have sincerely asked God for forgiveness, He's given you pardon.

GOD HAS THROWN ANY RECOLLECTION OF THIS INTO THE SEA OF FORGETFULNESS. The deed has been expunged from your record.

Always seeking God for wisdom, live your life making the best decisions that you can make for your own best interest. Be encouraged that every part of who you are makes a difference.

In beautiful fashion, at the end of the movie, Viola Davis' character, clothed in purple, was crowned and celebrated as Woman King. Know this. Within you lies the same kind of greatness. Like a Phoenix, rise up from the ashes of despair and claim who you are, Forgiven Woman. Yes, perhaps you (even with decisions that are not the proudest moments of your past) are too . . . a Woman King!

~Pastor Anna M. Jackson

TFT: What is something in your life experience that you haven't granted yourself forgiveness for? Once you finish today's steps, pray and ask God to heal you in this area.

My thoughts for today...

G.R.A.C.E.

Use the acronym G.R.A.C.E to reflect on today's lesson.

G. What are you most grateful for today?

_____

_____

R. As you reflect back on today's lesson, what remains on your mind and why?

_____

_____

A. What could YOU have done differently? What would need to change in order to get better results?

_____

_____

C. Commune - This is your time to pray and communicate with God. You can write it or say it aloud; but at least write down key points, so you can keep a record of your conversation and concern for God.

_____

_____

E. Based on today's lesson what action do you need to take?

_____

_____

You are a
WARRIOR
and you've been
equipped for this
FIGHT

NEW DAY OF G.R.A.C.E.

Day Seventeen

Your Life Has Benefits

Bless the Lord, O my soul,
And forget not all His benefits.
~ Psalm 103:2 (NKJV)~
(Minister Gamellia Davis -Contributing Author)

To "bless the Lord" means to praise, honor, and worship Him. And no matter what we may think or feel at times. . .there is always reason to bless the Lord!

Most of us have been taught to say "Thank you" when someone gives or does something for us. Keeping that in mind, remember, we have an obligation to bless the Lord!

Let's look at part two of today's verse. The meaning of benefits, according to Merriam-Webster dictionary, is something that produces good or helpful results or effects or that promotes well-being. Many decisions we make in life are based on the benefits we anticipate receiving and not always the consequences of our decisions. Actually, we should consider both, as the Bible tells us, to count up the cost. That's another lesson for another devotion.

Let's admit it, when we consider relationships, friendships, partnerships, jobs, careers, school choices, etc., the "what's in it for me" thought looms in our minds. It's human nature, and not to say we are not concerned for others, but we do it to protect ourselves.

I recall my first "real" job being my enlistment in the US Army. With this job came full health/medical, dental, vision, and life insurance benefits. Previously, I held part-time jobs, and worked during school, but never a full-time job with benefits. Being young and new on my own, I felt a sense of accomplishment to visit the doctor or dentist and leave without having to pay a bill. Not to mention, not receive a ton of bills afterward.

You see, the benefits package the military offered was great. Imagine how thrilled I was when a few years later when my family grew, those same benefits extended to each member of the family.

Fast forward a few more years, when I was out of the military, seeking my first civilian job. As you can imagine, I was looking for something with benefits very similar to what I received while serving. It's been 18 years since then, and even though I have work benefits today, they're not quite as inclusive and extensive as the ones I had become accustomed to in the military.

Now, I'm sure many of you reading this devotional are familiar with the period set aside each year for open enrollment; the time in which new benefits are to be confirmed or elected. Similarly, just as I was unsuccessful in finding civilian benefits comparable to those I had in the military, we run the same disappointment when we expect outside fulfillment to somehow be comparable to what God provides. You won't find anything that compares. Not even close.

God's open enrollment season is year-round and offers a lifetime of coverage. Yes, you read that correctly. . .A LIFETIME!

So, let's get back to the scripture. It tells us, "Bless the Lord . . . and forget not all HIS benefits."

God's benefits are not only His love, compassion, and understanding. Those expected or reciprocated gains we seek in relationships with others, God freely gives to us through our relationship with Him. A relationship with the Father encompasses every benefit we could desire from human relationships and more. Apart from His love, compassion, and understanding, God also offers the benefits of peace and joy, a covering, answered prayers, comfort, mercy, and most importantly GRACE! That alone is enough to thank Him for! ~Minister Gamellia Davis

TFT: Of all the BENEFITS God provides, what are you most grateful for?

My thoughts for today...

_____
_____
_____
_____
_____
_____
_____
_____
_____
_____
_____
_____
_____
_____
_____
_____
_____
_____
_____
_____
_____
_____
_____
_____

Conclude with G.R.A.C.E.

G.R.A.C.E.

Use the acronym G.R.A.C.E to reflect on today's lesson.

G. What are you most grateful for today?
_____
_____
_____

R. As you reflect back on today's lesson, what remains on your mind and why?
_____
_____

A. What could YOU have done differently? What would need to change in order to get better results?
_____
_____

C. Commune - This is your time to pray and communicate with God. You can write it or say it aloud; but at least write down key points, so you can keep a record of your conversation and concern for God.
_____
_____

E. Based on today's lesson what action do you need to take?
_____
_____

BLESS THE LORD, O MY SOUL, AND FORGET NOT ALL HIS BENEFITS

~Psalm 103:2~

Day Eighteen

GOD WASTES NOTHING

28 And we know that all things
work together for good to those who love God,
to those who are the called according to His purpose.
~Romans 8:28 (KJV)~

It's interesting how life circumstances seem like they consume us so quickly. One day it seems like we're just going about our day, living our life, happy and doing well in our families, marriages, careers, and other endeavors; and the next minute everything around us seems to be falling apart. What happened? Nothing is as it seemed. Relationships are strained. Stability in all forms seems unsure. Even for the most faithful of believers, it's difficult in those moments to remember or believe that God is in control and still has us in mind. I mean, if He did, why would He let us experience something like this...again. For some, the number of losses seems to outweigh the wins and gains. What happened to Jeremiah 29:11 which spoke about a hope and a future and not disaster for our lives?

Be encouraged, my friend. God's love and promises to us still exist. The Bible tells us in Isaiah 55:11 that God's word will never return to Him void. It will accomplish what He said that it would. That may not present itself in the world as perfection, but spiritually it does. God's will for our lives is perfect for us. And as a lover of God, you must remember that at ALL TIMES... ALL THINGS are WORKING TOGETHER for YOUR GOOD because you HAVE BEEN CALLED according to His PURPOSE. So, if in this moment you are discouraged by your circumstances or uncertain as to how a situation will work out for you, your spouse, children, or loved one...just repeat these words: "ALL THINGS ARE WORKING TOGETHER FOR THE GOOD." No matter what it looks like. "ALL THINGS ARE WORKING TOGETHER FOR THE GOOD." No matter what it feels like. "ALL THINGS ARE WORKING TOGETHER FOR THE GOOD." No matter what anyone has said. "ALL THINGS ARE WORKING TOGETHER FOR THE GOOD." No matter how dark the time might seem. "ALL THINGS ARE WORKING TOGETHER FOR THE GOOD."

Do you feel that in your spirit? I hope so. If not, repeat it a few more times. Believe it in your heart and confess it with your mouth. And if throughout today, or at any time, you begin to grow discouraged, remind yourself of the scripture and trust that even THIS is working together with everything God knows about your past and has planned for your future. Verse 29 Romans assures us that those God foreknew, He predestined (already determined by divine will), and those He predestined also called (purposed); whom He called, these He also justified (marked as good); and whom He justified, these He also glorified (elevated and made special something that was ordinary).

My dear friend, whatever things God has called you for, He's going to make certain that they are good so that your purpose will be fulfilled. In Jesus' name. Amen!

TFT: Recall a time now or previously when you knew God was working things together for your good.

My thoughts for today...

_____

_____

_____

_____

_____

_____

_____

_____

_____

_____

_____

_____

_____

_____

_____

_____

_____

_____

_____

_____

_____

_____

_____

_____

Conclude with G.R.A.C.E.

G.R.A.C.E.

Use the acronym G.R.A.C.E to reflect on today's lesson.

G. What are you most grateful for today?

_____

_____

_____

R. As you reflect back on today's lesson, what remains on your mind and why?

_____

_____

A. What could YOU have done differently? What would need to change in order to get better results?

_____

_____

C. Commune - This is your time to pray and communicate with God. You can write it or say it aloud; but at least write down key points, so you can keep a record of your conversation and concern for God.

_____

_____

E. Based on today's lesson what action do you need to take?

_____

_____

ALL THINGS

ARE WORKING

Together

FOR YOUR GOOD!

~ Romans 8:28 ~

Day Nineteen

Don't Worry About a Thing

Be anxious for nothing,
but in everything by prayer and supplication, with thanksgiving,
let your requests be made known to God;
7 and the peace of God, which surpasses all understanding,
will guard your hearts and minds through Christ Jesus.
~Philippians 4:6-7 (NKJV)~

This scripture is one that I recite to myself, as well as share with others possibly every day, and at a minimum once per week. It is one that my mother shared with me if I'm not mistaken when I was in college. I narrow it down to my college years because that was the time when I began to have real concerns about outcomes and decisions. Not just my own outcomes and decisions for myself, but outcomes and decisions for me that were in the hands of other people. Prior to college, all of my major life decisions lay in the balance of my parents. What I would wear for an occasion or whether I would or wouldn't participate in something. But when I got to college, professors, deans, and advisors had a stake in my fate...at least by position.

I was always active in church as a child and enjoyed going. But let me just be clear, when I got to college, needing to go to church to pray and be prayed for was a must. There were always these questions of whether I did the right thing, or whether I was in good standing or qualified enough for some program or organization I wanted to participate in or be considered for.

THE STRESS OF IT ALL!

In my college years was where I really began to trust God and understand what it meant to not only walk in obedience to Him and the benefits that brought; but also, what it meant to hear from God and receive His divine favor.

There were a few times within that four-year experience that I began experiencing MAJOR STRESS; especially regarding relationships and social involvement. Chaos and uncertainty seemed to distort everything that could have been good. Then in one of those times of expressing to my mother my difficulties with coping, she shared with me Philippians 4:6-7. The Good News Translation says this:

> *"Don't worry about anything,*
> *but in all your prayers ask God for what you need,*
> *always asking Him with a thankful heart."*

That part was pretty easy. I was truly grateful for every opportunity God had allowed and knew that He was the source behind the gifts and talents that allowed me to occupy the spaces I was afforded. But what I loved most about the scripture was the promise that it offered. The promise that I needed more than anything if I was going to complete the mission of earning a college education. Verse 7 said,

> *"And God's peace,*
> *which is far beyond human understanding,*
> *will keep your hearts and minds safe*
> *in union with Christ Jesus."*

God's peace is exactly what I needed to maneuver through the studies, the demands, and the relational encounters that I faced day-to-day, week-to-week, month-to-month, and year-to-year. Understand, I grew up as a country girl; so, going from spending most of my formative years as an only child to being on a college campus with thousands of people from all different backgrounds was undoubtedly exciting, but also spiritually draining. I needed something to keep me spiritually focused and astute. Philippians 4:6-7 did that. It reminded me of what the posture of my heart needed to be, and ideally where the peace from newfound trials would come from. God...and Him alone.

So today, remember if there is ever a time that you feel that your peace is being invaded and it's hard for you to concentrate on what it is that you know God has for you, pray from a posture of thankfulness, let God know what it is that you need, and then expect His peace to surround you.

Verse 8 follows by encouraging us to think about good and praiseworthy things, and that by doing so the God of peace will be with us. So then, if you're feeling alone or have thoughts that are negative, or if the stress of everything seems to be weighing on you... Ask yourself, "What are you thinking and consuming your thoughts with?" Our God is a God of peace, so you, my friend, don't have to worry about a thing.

———————————————

TFT: What area in your life, or in what situation, are you needing to experience God's peace?

My thoughts for today...

_____

_____

_____

_____

_____

_____

_____

_____

_____

_____

_____

_____

_____

_____

_____

_____

_____

_____

_____

_____

_____

_____

Conclude with G.R.A.C.E.

G.R.A.C.E.

Use the acronym G.R.A.C.E to reflect on today's lesson.

G. What are you most grateful for today?

_____

_____

_____

R. As you reflect back on today's lesson, what remains on your mind and why?

_____

_____

A. What could YOU have done differently? What would need to change in order to get better results?

_____

_____

C. Commune - This is your time to pray and communicate with God. You can write it or say it aloud; but at least write down key points, so you can keep a record of your conversation and concern for God.

_____

_____

E. Based on today's lesson what action do you need to take?

_____

_____

And the peace of God,
which transcends
all understanding,
will guard your hearts
and your minds
in Christ Jesus.
~Philippians 4:7~

Day Twenty

Your Future Will Be Greater

*6 Now there was a day when the sons of God came to present themselves
before the Lord, and Satan also came among them.
7 And the Lord said to Satan, "From where do you come?"
So Satan answered the Lord and said,
"From going to and fro on the earth, and from walking back and forth on it."
8 Then the Lord said to Satan, "Have you considered My servant Job,
that there is none like him on the earth,
a blameless and upright man, one who fears God and shuns evil?"
~Job 1:6-8 (KJV)~*

Since Satan was cast down from Heaven, he's been doing
what he does - going from here and there seeking whom he
can devour [prey upon and destroy] (Peter 5:8). The
scripture here in Job 1:8, when Satan answered God as to
what he had been doing, God asked him if he had
considered trying his servant Job; describing him as
blameless and upright and emphasizing that there were
none as righteous as him in all the earth.

Wow! Isn't it interesting that God suggested that His best be
tested? I believe now after completing the Book of Job that
God from the very beginning knew not only how Job would
respond and that he would make it through the trial, but He
also was fully aware of the greatness He had in store for Job
on the other side of his test. Job 42:17 accounts that the Lord
blessed the latter days of Job more than his beginning.
Could I get you to believe that about the trials you've faced
or are currently facing? Don't fret. Not only does Satan have
to answer to God, but he has no authority to go beyond what
God allows. Your trial will not only strengthen you and

prepare you for the blessing God has ahead for you; but it will also encourage your family and others who know you, even when at times they too may doubt that God will deliver you.

Job 22:28-30 AMP says,

"You will also decide and decree a thing,
and it will be established for you;
And the light [of God's favor] will shine upon your ways. When you
are cast down and humbled,
you will speak with confidence,
And the humble person He will lift up and save.
He will even rescue the one [for whom you intercede]
who is not innocent;
And he will be rescued
through the cleanness of your hands."

Today, put your whole confidence in the Lord. Recall the scripture that reminds us not to fear or worry, because the Lord will never leave us or abandon us altogether (Hebrews 13:6). Regardless of where we might find ourselves, there is nothing that we can ever do, feel, or think that would cause God to forsake us. Yes, there may be times when we may feel distant from Him because of our own actions or because of how down we might be, but the truth is God is still near. So stand in confidence knowing that God is your Father. He will establish you as you walk with Him and trust Him with your future. Even when you are in distress or weary, you can still know and speak with confidence that God is still your God. Today's scripture tells us that our God will even rescue those we intercede for, even when they are not necessarily innocent. Remember that's not our call to worry about or to judge. God has a plan for those we pray for just as He does for us. So, keep in mind that someone connected to you will receive favor or be rescued because of their connection with you and your connection with Christ. When you make your decision and decree today, know that what God is establishing is not just for you. It is also for those He's entrusted to you based on your relationship with them. Yes! Your faith and faithfulness are healing and delivering the bloodline.

TFT: Whom do you know that God has entrusted to you that your faith is used for their benefit? Don't forget to pray for them today and that God will discipline you and strengthen you to continue to intercede on their behalf.

My thoughts for today...

_____

_____

_____

_____

_____

_____

_____

_____

_____

_____

_____

_____

_____

_____

_____

_____

_____

_____

_____

_____

_____

_____

_____

_____

_____

Conclude with G.R.A.C.E.

G.R.A.C.E.

Use the acronym G.R.A.C.E to reflect on today's lesson.

G. What are you most grateful for today?
_____
_____
_____

R. As you reflect back on today's lesson, what remains on your mind and why?
_____
_____

A. What could YOU have done differently? What would need to change in order to get better results?
_____
_____

C. Commune - This is your time to pray and communicate with God. You can write it or say it aloud; but at least write down key points, so you can keep a record of your conversation and concern for God.
_____
_____

E. Based on today's lesson what action do you need to take?
_____
_____

Day Twenty-One

Welcome to Your New Place

Watch for the new thing I am going to do.
It is happening already—you can see it now!
I will make a road through the wilderness
and give you streams of water there.
~Isaiah 43:19 (GNT)~

Now, I bet you didn't actually realize how many different scriptures there are in the Bible that make reference to newness. You shouldn't be surprised at all, though. As I've mentioned before, God is not merely a creator, but He is THE Creator. And if I know anything about creators, they are constantly driven to create.

In fact, I consider myself a creator. I dance, sing a little, play the piano, enjoy cooking, craft, write. . . You get my drift. But what I'm trying to convey is that as a creator, my mind never stops thinking of what's next, and I've been told that this is common for most other creators as well. So, if in human form, the "typical" creator is constantly seeking to make new things, how much more would we consider our Heavenly Father's desire to create something new in us?

Oh gosh! The thought just made me so excited!

For me, each day when I get up I am thinking about what I want to do to contribute to myself, my family, my calling and purpose, my community, and to the greatness of the Kingdom. When I go to bed (and it's hard at times), I'm still thinking about what I need to do to complete certain tasks and bring them to fruition the next day. But can we actually grasp the brevity of the fact that God never sleeps nor slumbers and He's THE Creator?

Can you imagine how much He is considering concerning the children that He loves in the place that He created from nothing? Oh goodness! I'm saying, "God! Pick me! I'm ready! I'm right here!"

The scripture says that what God is going to do, He's doing already; so much to the fact that He is going to make roads through the wilderness and provide water there. Well, some versions of the scripture describe it specifically as roads through the desert. . . and supply water. . . in the desert. . .the dry place.

Have you ever been to or witnessed the desert? I sure have. And let me just tell you. . . You ain't experienced hot and dry until you've either lived or spent substantial time in the desert. The vegetation or topical features in the desert are vastly different from what you'd find in climates that experience regular precipitation. The desert renders sand upon sand, sand dunes, sand storms, tumbleweeds, and cacti. The likelihood of stumbling upon a creek or pond randomly sprinkled in the desert is unlikely, based on my experience.

If you're not used to it, the desert changes you. You see differently. You sweat differently. Heck, I even thought differently.

For me, the fact that I have an actual real-life reference point to the attributes of a desert makes this scripture more palpable for me.

The scripture says in Isaiah 43:19 that God is going to do a new thing in the place that is not only perceivably dry, but if we describe it in terms of being the wilderness, it further means that this place is uncultivated, uninhabited, empty and pathless.

Listen! I just got excited again!

By definition, THIS PLACE is meant for only you. No one has been here before; and God intentionally purposed it with you in mind, so that you and anyone who sees you on the other side of THIS PLACE will know that only God could have given you directions here.

I referred to this also in the 5-Day Morning COFFEE Devotion that my favorite part of the wilderness definition is the part about it being uninhabitED – no one is here. But, it didn't say it was uninhabitABLE - incapable of being occupied. THIS PLACE is yours for the taking. You've got some room and some freedom to do some things.

Be encouraged and lean into grace. This new place where you've found yourself has been previously unoccupied by anyone so that you can make your mark. The Creator is giving you some autonomy to create the vision you've dreamed about. Might I suggest. . . Use all your colors and make them beautiful. Then, with the streams of water that are there, DRINK UP and take some to-go. This won't be the end of your journey.

TFT: Reflect on what feels different about your NEW PLACE?

My thoughts for today...

_____
_____
_____
_____
_____
_____
_____
_____
_____
_____
_____
_____
_____
_____
_____
_____
_____
_____
_____
_____
_____
_____
_____
_____
_____
_____

Conclude with G.R.A.C.E.

G.R.A.C.E.

Use the acronym G.R.A.C.E to reflect on today's lesson.

G. What are you most grateful for today?

_____

_____

_____

R. As you reflect back on today's lesson, what remains on your mind and why?

_____

_____

A. What could YOU have done differently? What would need to change in order to get better results?

_____

_____

C. Commune - This is your time to pray and communicate with God. You can write it or say it aloud; but at least write down key points, so you can keep a record of your conversation and concern for God.

_____

_____

E. Based on today's lesson what action do you need to take?

_____

_____

Watch for the
NEW THING
I am going to do.
It is happening already—
YOU CAN SEE IT NOW!
I will make a road
through the wilderness
and give you
streams of water there.

~Isaiah 43:19~

Conclusion

Whatever You Hope...God is Able

Now unto him that is able to do exceeding abundantly above all that we ask or think, according to the power that worketh in us,
~Ephesians 3:20 (KJV)~

You've been on this New Day journey for 21 days, and today is the day that you completely take the reigns and responsibility to trust God for the life that has been destined for you in this next season and beyond.

Let me encourage you to hold back nothing. Whatever it is that God has placed in you that is pressing upon your belly to release, be brave and obedient to do it.

Ephesians 3:20, I believe, is the perfect scripture to use as a reminder of the true power and sovereignty of God to not only do something new in us . . . but also to perform it to a level we can't even fathom.

The point I'd like to leave with you from the scripture is the fact that there is no punctuation. I've shared this observation before; so, you may find it in one of my previous blogs or sermons, and I think I even mentioned it in the 5-Day Morning C.O.F.F.E.E. Devotion. But, I reiterate the detail of the missing punctuation (though some may not notice or care) because punctuation as you might know is crucial to a sentence's structure as well as how it is interpreted and conceptualized.

When I read that God is able to do exceedingly. . . abundantly. . . above. . . all. . . It just helps me to realize that God's abilities to perform greatness for us and through us keeps going and going, and getting better and better. So much better that what manifests is not just greater than we can ask, but also more than we can think; according to the power that worketh in us. And the power that works in us is God's power anyway. So it's a win-win.

Here's to winning in this new season. Today is your New Day. . . and each day after this one is just as new. Remember that! Now, BEHOLD! God is doing a NEW THING!

TFT: Use your reflection time and pages to outline how you will maneuver and show up in this next season. What commitment do you need to make to God, yourself, and others?

My thoughts for today...

_____

_____

_____

_____

_____

_____

_____

_____

_____

_____

_____

_____

_____

_____

_____

_____

_____

_____

_____

_____

_____

_____

_____

_____

_____

Conclude with G.R.A.C.E.

G.R.A.C.E.

Use the acronym G.R.A.C.E to reflect on the final lesson.

G. What are you most grateful for today?

_____
_____
_____

R. As you reflect back on today's lesson, what remains on your mind and why?

_____
_____

A. What could YOU have done differently? What would need to change in order to get better results?

_____
_____

C. Commune - This is your time to pray and communicate with God. You can write it or say it aloud; but at least write down key points, so you can keep a record of your conversation and concern for God.

_____
_____

E. Based on today's lesson what action do you need to take?

_____
_____

dawn's reminder

Even when your season changes, REMEMBER... You can still BLOOM.

APPENDIX A

New Day of G.R.A.C.E.
Quick Scripture References

The Bible is divided into two main sections, the Old Testament and the New Testament. The Old Testament contains 39 books, and the New Testament contains 27. The books are arranged in the Bible according to their historical and chronological order.

For your convenience and reference, here is a list of scriptures used throughout the lessons. You will find them in both Biblical order (according to their place in the Bible) and then according to their focus (Faith, Hope, Love, Encouragement, etc.).

Use these scriptures to refer back to from time to time to help you stay connected to God's Holy Word.

"Your word I have hidden in my heart, that I might not sin against You."
~Psalm 119:11

Old Testament:

Genesis 1:1-5
Exodus 33:14
Psalm 23
Psalm 46:5
Psalm 73:26

Psalm 100:5
Psalms 37:25
Proverbs 3:5-6
Habakkuk 1:1-5

New Testament:

Matthew 5:6
Matthew 6:33
Matthew 14:20
Mark 11:24
Luke 1:38
Romans 8:28-29
1 Corinthians 10:13
2 Corinthians 5:17
2 Corinthians 12:9

Ephesians 2:8-10
Ephesians 3:20
Ephesians 6:10
Philippians 1:6
Philippians 4:6-7
Hebrew 13:5-6
1 Peter 5:8

Here is a list of the lessons' scriptures according to their focus. These scriptures can provide encouragement, comfort, and guidance during difficult times; and, with meditation and prayer, can help to overcome fear, doubt, and uncertainty.

Faith:
Matthew 6:33
Mark 11:24
2 Corinthian 5:17
Ephesians 2:8-10

Hope:
Lamentations 3:22-23
Psalm 51:12
Psalm 100:5
Psalm 103:2
Isaiah 40:31
Matthew 5:6
Matthew 14:20
Romans 8:28-29
Ephesians 3:20
Philippians 1:6

Love:
Psalm 103:12
1 Corinthians 10:13
Philippians 4:6-7

Peace:
Psalm 46:5
Philippians 4:6-9

Patience:
Philippians 4:6
James 1:4

Strength:
Nehemiah 8:10
Psalm 73:26
Ephesians 6:10

Encouragement:
Job 1:6-8
Job 22:28-30
Psalm 46:5
Proverbs 3:5-6
Hebrews 13:6

Courage:
Ephesians 6:10
Exodus 33:14
Isaiah 40:31
Peter 5:8

Trust:
Psalm 20:7
Psalm 46:5
Proverbs 3:5-6
Isaiah 55:10-11
Hebrew 13:5-6

Overcoming Fear, Doubt, & Uncertainty:
Psalm 46:5:
James 1:4
Philippians 4:6-7
Proverbs 3:5-6
Isaiah 43:19

Change/Transformation:
Isaiah 43:19
2 Corinthian 5:17 (KJV)

Fruits of the Spirit
Galatian 5:22

Obedience
Luke 1:38 (KJV)

APPENDIX B

Special Acknowledgements

Acknowledgements

A New Day of GRACE has been a labor of love.

HOW I GOT HERE - My intent, after releasing the 5-Day Morning C.O.F.F.E.E. Devotion in September 2021, was to write a new devotional by March 2022. My plan was to have it just in time for Women's History Month. However, 2022 took a different turn. The momentum of the children's book Heeeyy Dandelion took off and brought the 5-Day Morning C.O.F.F.E.E. Devotion along with it, and things didn't slow down again (somewhat) until September of 2022.

I have come to realize that God's timing is always perfect. He allowed me the time and space to complete it and gave me the perfect title. Plus, God allowed me to understand His grace from a greater perspective. He had already given me the title New Day, and that is exemplary of everything else He's given me, but. . .it needed the element of grace as well. And so, NOW is the time.

WHO I WOULD LIKE TO THANK - I would like to start my acknowledgments this time with my husband. He has been instrumental in allowing me to be the best I can be in the author and ministry space. I couldn't show up the way I do without his love and support.

Then I would like to thank my children, Rudy and Anasia, for being champions in their own way. Some people know this already, but Rudy and I are very close, and I run a lot of my creative thoughts by him before I present them. I trust his insight on most things. God blessed Him with a wealth of

148

wisdom from a very young age, and I'm just glad that he thinks enough of me as his mother, a minister, as well as a fellow creative to take the time to help me along this journey.

Anasia wants to be my mini-me. Because of that, she tries hard to understand my projects and to help me. She's one of my biggest cheerleaders and promoters. I can't tell you how many times I've gone to a school open house, parent-teacher conference, or even the grocery store, and someone approaches me about what Anasia has told them her mommy is doing. There will be a place on the payroll for you, Anasia, one day.

Thanks to my parents, Garland and Lynda Spivey, for loving and supporting me. It feels good to know that you're both proud of me and that you share my efforts with all your friends. Everything that I do is somehow a reflection of what you all instilled in me all those years ago. I still strive to make you proud.

Finally, I want to thank my hometown, Mansfield, LA. From the most seasoned of you, all the way to the younger generation, you all never cease to amaze me. Thank you all for supporting me, recognizing me, and championing me. It means more than you'll ever know. And even though some people jokingly say it now, know this…I'll never get "too big" to call Mansfield home.

Special Dedication

Memorial Dedication

When I began my acknowledgments, I said that I had outlined plans for 2022, but the events of the year took some unexpected turns. One of the most major turns was the loss of my father. So, I want to include a special dedication to him as well.

To: Daddy

Though distance sometimes separated us, both figuratively and literally, the love I had in my heart for you is hard to explain in words.

It makes me feel good to know that I made you proud. My only regret is that I didn't know the complete fabric of who you were. Maybe it's assumed that some things are not meant for a girl to know about her daddy, or maybe you thought some things wouldn't interest me. I wish you would have told or shown me anyway; because, now I feel like I missed some precious opportunities that I didn't know were there. But I at least know now (from the remarks given at your memorial by those who respected you and called you friend) that I'm actually more like you than I ever knew. All the good parts. And honestly . . . That's all that matters. The other parts have been forgotten and forgiven.

With that said, I dedicate this book to you, Daddy - the late,
Charlie Charleston, Jr.
02/25/1954 - 05/24/2022

Daddy, I'm so glad that we finally had a chance to see a New Day, and that God graced me to be with you in your final days. I love you always, ~Nikki (Dawn Nikole)

APPENDIX C

Extra Journaling Pages

G.R.A.C.E.

G. What are you most grateful for today?

_____

_____

_____

R. As you reflect back on today's lesson, what remains on your mind and why?

_____

_____

A. What could YOU have done differently? What would need to change in order to get better results?

_____

_____

C. Commune - This is your time to pray and communicate with God. You can write it or say it aloud; but at least write down key points, so you can keep a record of your conversation and concern for God.

_____

_____

E. Based on today's lesson what action do you need to take?

_____

_____

My thoughts for today...

G.R.A.C.E.

G. What are you most grateful for today?

_____

_____

_____

R. As you reflect back on today's lesson, what remains on your mind and why?

_____

_____

A. What could YOU have done differently? What would need to change in order to get better results?

_____

_____

C. Commune - This is your time to pray and communicate with God. You can write it or say it aloud; but at least write down key points, so you can keep a record of your conversation and concern for God.

_____

_____

E. Based on today's lesson what action do you need to take?

_____

_____

My thoughts for today...

G.R.A.C.E.

G. What are you most grateful for today?
_____
_____
_____

R. As you reflect back on today's lesson, what remains on your mind and why?
_____
_____

A. What could YOU have done differently? What would need to change in order to get better results?
_____
_____

C. Commune - This is your time to pray and communicate with God. You can write it or say it aloud; but at least write down key points, so you can keep a record of your conversation and concern for God.
_____
_____

E. Based on today's lesson what action do you need to take?
_____
_____

My thoughts for today...

G.R.A.C.E.

G. What are you most grateful for today?
_____
_____
_____

R. As you reflect back on today's lesson, what remains on your mind and why?
_____
_____

A. What could YOU have done differently? What would need to change in order to get better results?
_____
_____

C. Commune - This is your time to pray and communicate with God. You can write it or say it aloud; but at least write down key points, so you can keep a record of your conversation and concern for God.
_____
_____

E. Based on today's lesson what action do you need to take?
_____
_____

My thoughts for today...

G.R.A.C.E.

G. What are you most grateful for today?

_____

_____

_____

R. As you reflect back on today's lesson, what remains on your mind and why?

_____

_____

A. What could YOU have done differently? What would need to change in order to get better results?

_____

_____

C. Commune - This is your time to pray and communicate with God. You can write it or say it aloud; but at least write down key points, so you can keep a record of your conversation and concern for God.

_____

_____

E. Based on today's lesson what action do you need to take?

_____

_____

My thoughts for today...

APPENDIX D

About the Authors

Multiple award-winning author **DAWN CHARLESTON-GREEN** - a native of Mansfield, LA, currently residing in Grovetown, GA - led and compiled *New Day of G.R.A.C.E.*, which is the second published devotional in her writing repertoire.

Dawn is both a wife and mother, as well as Veteran Army Officer, minister, mentor, life-blogger, entrepreneur, self-published author, speaker, and publishing coach. Dawn's messages and ministry focus on women, youth, marriages, and families. Her professional background includes education, counseling, and child advocacy.

Dawn is also the founder, creator, and CEO of Dawn of New Day 365, LLC. The DND365 movement focuses on women journeying through everyday life; providing content, conversations, and inspiration.

Dawn is a graduate of Northwestern State University of Louisiana, where she received a Bachelor of Arts in English in 1996 and a Master of Education in Counseling in 2003. She is 12 hours shy of a doctoral degree in Educational Leadership.

Dawn and her husband, Leon, have a blended family of six children. and serve together as ministry leaders for the R.O.C.K. Ministries.

AUTHOR | SPEAKER | MINISTER

For more of Dawn's writings go to www.dawnofanewday365.com.
Join the Dawn of a New Day 365 Women's Facebook Group and follow on all social media platforms.

LEON J. GREEN, JR.

PASTOR | LEADER | TEACHER

Elder Green serves as the Pastor of Reaching and Restoring Others for Christ Kingdom Ministries (R.O.C.K.). He is an avid preacher, teacher, and mentor with an unwavering commitment to restoring holiness among God's people. Through his calling and ministry, Leon seeks to provide guidance on how to grow spiritually through prayer, meditation, scripture reading and discernment.

Elder Green considers himself a life-long learner. He has earned multiple degrees, including a Bachelor of Science in Business Administration; a Master of Science in Project Management; and is in the final phase of completion of his Ph.D. in Business Administration.

Leon has written articles to bring encouragement and insight for Still Waters International Ministry, as well as to his wife's platform, Dawn of a New Day 365.

Elder Leon Green and his wife, Dawn, have a blended family of six children: Shatira, Leon III, Rudy, Gabrielle, Taylor, and Anasia. And Leon is a grandfather to 10 grandchildren.

Find Pastor Green's contribution to this devotion on *Day Twelve*, ***Never Forsaken.***

ELDER LEON GREEN, JR. is a native of New Orleans, LA. After leaving New Orleans, he joined the United States Army and served for 29 years; retiring as a Command Sergeant Major.

Elder Green has become known for his unquenchable passion to see the glory of Jesus Christ strongly and suitably manifested in the lives of the broken through the comprehensive gospel.

Leon is an ordained licensed minister of the gospel and committed to developing both new saints and men in ministry.

Join in virtually to
Reaching & **R**estoring **O**ther for
Christ **K**ingdom Ministries
(R.O.C.K.)
THUR @6:30PM EST and SUN
@10AM EST
ZOOM ID: 745-157-4570
Passcode: Faith

Gamellia Davis

MINISTER GAMELLIA F. DAVIS is a wife, mother, and minister originally from Colerain, North Carolina (a small town off the coast of Eastern North Carolina), but currently resides in Ladson, South Carolina.

Gamellia is married to husband Cwinton Davis and is mother to son Jamal (21) and daughter Jamiah (19) Davis, both of who are college students currently.

Minister Davis has worked in Higher Education Administration for over 20 years and currently serves as the Director of Finance at a local community college in Charleston, South Carolina.

Gamellia obtained a Bachelor of Science in Accounting from The University of North Carolina at Greensboro and a Master of Business Administration from Limestone College.

Gamellia is a proud Veteran of the United States Army. Of her many roles, being a child of God means the most. She is a Licensed Minister who enjoys working with youth and serving and assisting in any capacity.

In ministry, Gamellia has served as a Sunday School Teacher, Youth Department Director, and Women's Ministry Leader. She also ministers and teaches the Gospel for Sunday

Gamellia is often called upon to organize church conferences and retreats, and shares her gifts for organization and creativity freely with others.

Gamellia's hobbies include completing jigsaw puzzles, reading, and spending time with family.

Find Minister Davis' contribution to *New Day of G.R.A.C.E.* on *Day Seventeen.*

ANNA MORRIS JACKSON is a lifelong resident of Mansfield, Louisiana. Her background includes being a pastor and retired educator.

Pastor Jackson has two adult daughters, Anitra Collins and Donna Hadley, and through them is the mother-in-love to bonus sons Billy and Kevin.

Aside from her children, Anna has four grandchildren: Anna Elise, Zion Michael, Aaron Joseph, and Reagan Victoria. Hadley. Anna Elise and her husband Deatric, are parents of Dorian Wayne Thomas, Anaa's first great grandson.

Anna graduated with distinction from DeSoto High School in 1968. She received her BA and M.Ed. from Louisiana State University - Shreveport, and also did post graduate studies at LSU - Baton Rouge.

Anna Jackson retired in 2014 from the Caddo Parish School System of Louisiana after 39 ½ years as an educator; beginning her journey in education as a school secretary. Once she completed her degree, Anna went on to become a 5th and 6th Grade English and Reading teacher. She completed her career as a 7th and 8th Grade English and Reading teacher at Keithville Elementary Middle School.

As an educator, Anna was passionate about helping students pursue excellence and leadership at a young age. During her tenure, her peers nominated her for the Teacher of the Year and her students recommended her and secured her a spot for Who's Who in Teachers.

Pastor Jackson received her first pastoral assignment in the United Methodist Church in 2005. In 2009 she was appointed to and currently serves as the proud Senior Pastor of Wesley UMC Mansfield, LA.

Pastor Anna completed the Methodist Conference Course of Study School through the satellite campuses of Southern Methodist University's Perkins School of Theology; first, at the Lon Morris College; then, First United Methodist Church, Jacksonville, TX; and finally, at First United Methodist, Lufkin, Texas.

This year Pastor Jackson reaches mandatory retirement. She will continue to serve as a retired pastor.

Pastor Jackson's contribution to *New Day of G.R.A.C.E.* can be found on *Day Sixteen* entitled **You've Been Forgiven**.

PASTOR | LEADER | EDUCATOR

ANNA MORRIS JACKSON

172

ASHLEY THOMAS

MINISTER | AUTHOR | CREATIVE

MINISTER ASHLEY THOMAS is a Self-Published Author & Breakthrough Strategist, Creative Mindset Coach, Owner/CEO of ThaVine Revelations LLC, and the founder of Ashley Thomas Creative Academy. However, before anything else, she is a Woman of God.

As an Ordained Minister, Ashley obtained her Associate's Degree in Biblical Studies and Chaplaincy, alongside her husband, in 2020.

Inspired by a life of transformation of her own, she has also authored several books and journals, including but not limited to:

- Something Has Got To Break

- Jesus Knows My Battles 31-Day Anxiety Challenge

- Seek God, Slay Goals - Prayer Journal

- She is Armed and Dangerous Prayer Journal

- Real. Men. Pray. Prayer Journal

Outside of her spiritual gifts and love for God's people, Minister Ashley has a talent and passion for creating. Years ago, God used her creativity to help her through some of her most challenging times while she and her children lived in a program for homeless women and children. During that time, she would use her God-given creative gifts to interact with and encourage the other residents. This planted the seed of what has now blossomed into her passion for mentoring women. She now walks in this calling with her *Breakthrough with Ashley Mentorship and Community Program*, providing Biblical life skills and strategies to help women break free from the bondage of the past.

With blessings and breakthroughs of her own, Ashley also teaches women of faith, who are passionate about creating, how to use their God-gifted talents to help others through their business or ministry.

Minster Ashley wrote the foreword for *New Day of G.R.A.C.E.* and also contributed on *Day Seven* entitled ***Go Ahead. Ask!***

RUDOLPH A. VALENTINE, III is the son of lead author, Dawn Charleston-Green. He is co-author and the inspiration behind the award-winning children's book *Rudy the Smart Kid,* also published by Dawn of a New Day 365 Publishing in 2023.

Born in Augusta, Georgia, Rudy grew up as a military brat living in Georgia, Louisiana, and Texas. He graduated in the top 15% and was the Class President of his class from Grovetown High School in 2016.

Rudy also grew up as a P.K. (preacher's kid); as his mother, Dawn and bonus dad, Leon, were leaders and ordained ministers in ministry. As his parents served, Rudy spent his formative years participating in church plays, praise dancing, and serving as the drummer for the choir and praise team. He also was often called upon to minister messages to the youth and men's ministries.

Apart from his academics and church activities, Rudy was also a stellar athlete; playing both basketball and participating in Track & Field. He was top-ranked in the State of Georgia in both the long and triple jump.

Rudy attended The Grambling State University and was a member of the Men's Track & Field Team; having been a part of the 2017 SWAC Championship Men's Outdoor Team.

EMCEE | COMEDIAN| AUTHOR

RUDY VALENTINE, III

While in college, Rudy continued to excel in academics and leadership, and was inducted into GSU's Earl Lester Cole Honors College and the National Society of Leadership and Success. Rudy received his Bachelor of Arts in Mass Communication in 2020.

Rudy currently resides in Houston, Texas where he is a Content Creator, Emcee, the Founder & CEO of GOATGANG ENTERTAINMENT, LLC., and now a two-time author.

Rudy's contribution to New Day of G.R.A.C.E. can be found on *Day Fifteen - **Strength & Conditioning**.*

Connect With the Author

INTERESTED IN CONNECTING WITH AWARD-WINNING AUTHOR DAWN CHARLESTON-GREEN?

For speaking engagements and collaborations, reach out to Dawn on any of her fields of expertise, which include: **Resiliency - The Art of Repurposing After a Setback**; or framework in the areas of Leadership, Children's Mental Health and Educational Advocacy, Women's Empowerment, Ministry (Marriage and Family), Self-Care; Friendship and MORE.

In addition to both of Dawn's devotions, she has taught and facilitated women's groups for over two decades. Dawn is passionate about women becoming intentional about communing with God daily.

BOOK DAWN CHARLESTON-GREEN FOR YOUR WOMEN'S GROUP OR CONFERENCE.

Apart from devotions, Dawn is also an award-winning children's book author. For more information, or to request an **Author Visit** for your SCHOOL or YOUTH GROUP, go to **www.heeeyydandelion.com/about.**

For more information from Dawn Charleston-Green and Dawn of a New Day 365 Life Blog and Creations, make sure to subscribe to
DAWN OF A NEW DAY 365
www.dawnofanewday365.com.

Join the Dawn of a New Day 365 movement today, so you don't miss anything. You can also follow Dawn of New Day 365 on Facebook, YouTube, Instagram, and Pinterest. Use this QR code to connect and catch up on the latest.

DO YOU HAVE A STORY TO TELL?

If you've written a story or have one in mind, but don't know how to go from idea to published, Dawn would love to help you bring your story to life. Let the DND365 Rising Author Academy help you with writing, editing, copyrighting, publishing, and preliminary marketing.

YOU TOO CAN BE A PUBLISHED AUTHOR.

Or, are you a previously published author who wants to take the lead on your distribution and marketing? Consulting Services are also available.

BOOK a discovery call today by using the QR code, or EMAIL dawnofanewday365@yahoo.com.

Made in the USA
Columbia, SC
23 January 2024

30177726R00111